the MINISTRY *of* MARRIAGE

Jim Binney

FAITHFUL LIFE PUBLISHERS
North Fort Myers, FL
FaithfulLifePublishers.com

The Ministry of Marriage

© 2014 by Jim Binney
ISBN: 978-1-63073-057-4

Published and printed by:
Faithful Life Publishers • North Fort Myers, FL 33903
888.720.0950 • info@FaithfulLifePublishers.com
www.FaithfulLifePublishers.com

NOTE: The fact that materials produced by other publishers may be referred to in this volume does not constitute an endorsement by Faithful Life Publishers of the content or theological position of materials produced by such publishers.

All Scripture is quoted from the Authorized King James Version.

Printed in the United States of America

19 18 17 16 15 14   3 4 5 6 7

DEDICATION

To my loving wife, Maria, whose constant
devotion and loving companionship
has ministered so wonderfully to me.
I love you Babe!

AUTHOR'S NOTE:

I ask the reader's understanding in any
references to my wife Sandra who is now in Heaven.
This book was initially written before her departure
and therefore reflects our prior relationship.

TABLE OF CONTENTS

FOREWORD

Every once in a while, someone approaches an old subject with a new perspective that opens up a whole new vista in understanding. After many years of counseling couples who are having marital difficulties because of a misunderstanding of what marriage really is, Jim Binney has discovered what I believe is the key element that is missing in these marriages: the concept of *ministry*. *The Ministry of Marriage* is especially refreshing because few people, even marriage counselors, seem to understand the importance of ministry in a marriage.

While this may seem like a novel idea to many readers, in reality it is not. As Dr. Binney points out succinctly in this book, Scripture teaches that ministry should be the underlying, fundamental reason for marriage. So many marriages are based on feelings and an incorrect concept of what love is that it is no wonder they are falling apart. For a building to stand, it must have a good foundation. A marriage partner who believes that his mate owes him something and is not meeting his perceived needs is doomed to be disappointed because he does not understand why he should have gotten married in the first place. A person is not supposed to get married in order to be ministered unto but to minister.

Some things are learned and understood only by experience, and the years of experience that Dr. Binney has had in counseling couples gives him first-hand information concerning the subject at hand. This author not only addresses the problems people face today but his experience also enables him to present the solutions that must be implemented to save a marriage from being dashed on the rocks of a false concept of what marriage is all about.

There are three concepts among the many presented in *The Ministry of Marriage* that stand out in my mind as elements that will transform a marriage in difficulty. One is developing a proper view of God, who He is, and what He is like. Almost every problem we face has its solution in a proper view of God, and this concept applies to marriage as well. Couples who gain a right view of God have taken the first step in solving the difficulties they face with getting along together in the way God planned.

The second concept is one that has been neglected in modern-day understanding and counseling: the biblical analogy between a marriage and the relationship between Christ and His church. A proper understanding and application of this doctrine will transform any marriage to which it is applied. When God chose to use this analogy, He was giving us His standard and purpose for establishing the institutions of marriage and family. Even the prevailing misunderstanding and corruption of God's purpose for sex can be cleared up by applying this doctrine, both before and after a couple is married.

The third concept that *The Ministry of Marriage* makes clear is an understanding of what love is. The modern concept of love, even among many Christians, is so distorted and distant from God's concept that no marriage based on this false concept can survive the pressures that modern society and the world place on it. Dr. Binney's analysis and correct teaching will give hope and understanding to the partners in any marriage relationship, even if there are no problems within the marriage. Those who are having trouble will find the path to discovery and those whose marriages are already stable will gain new insight that will make their marriages even stronger.

In my more than forty years of trying to counsel married couples, I have never read a book that more clearly dissects the difficulties that married couples face and then more succinctly provides the solutions and steps necessary for a marriage to be what God intended for it to be. Anyone who reads this book will find hope for himself and for the one that God has intended to be "closer than a brother," closer than any other human relationship we will ever know.

Frank Garlock

INTRODUCTION

Y̲ou are reading this book for a reason: maybe you desire to find help for a frustrating marriage. You may hope to improve an already good marriage. Or maybe you are on the verge of making a life-changing decision about whether to continue in your marriage. Perhaps you even want to understand more about marriage before entering into it. Whatever the reason, there is help for you here.

There is also some basic information you need to know as you approach this book. For a decade and a half, I have counseled marriages at the Moorehead Manor on the estate of the late Agnes Moorehead (best known for her role as Endora in the television series *Bewitched*). We are doing the Lord's work in a witch's house, but then stranger things have happened. When couples arrive for marriage counseling, I conduct an orientation session with them. I explain to them what they can expect during the week of counseling. Welcome to the reader's "orientation session."

CHRIST-CENTERED SOLUTIONS

First, the emphasis will be on Christ-centered, God-focused solutions. You have most likely already tried some of the popular psychological theories and found them wanting. The reason for this is that they have failed to address the deepest need of your marriage. If it is true that "I can do all things through Christ," it is also true that "without me ye can do nothing." The Lord Jesus Christ has never been an "add-on" to relationships for the believer. He is the relationship. Our goal is to bring Christ back to His rightful place at the very center of marriage.

BIBLE-BASED STEPS OF RESOLUTION

Second, you can expect to find Bible-based steps of resolution to your present questions about marriage. Christ is the Answer, but if you have tried to find Him as the answer to your pressing needs, and have been disappointed and frustrated in your search, it may be because you have overlooked the steps of resolution. Yes, Christ is the answer! He is where you need to be! His presence is what you long for, and His power is available. But He is there and you are here. The question is how to get from where you are to where He is. That journey is the resolution. This book will provide your biblical, step-by-step principles that will lead you to Him! Confusing the solution with the steps of resolution has frustrated and discouraged many seekers of truth. Jesus is not only the Living Word but the Written Word as well. *"Behold, I have come—In the volume of the book."* And it is in the pages of the Word of God that He reveals how to be *"conformed to the image of Christ."*

A BIBLICAL WORLDVIEW OF MARRIAGE, LOVE, AND SEX

Many Christians seem to get their notions of love from the Love Boat instead of the Love Book. They get their ideas of marriage from romance novels instead of the Bible and their notions of sex from the *Playboy* philosophy instead of the pages of Scripture. In all probability you have borrowed from some of these sources in forming your own views about marriage. It is the challenge of believers everywhere, and especially Christian partners of the marriage union, to refuse to conform to the thinking of the world and replace worldly philosophies with biblical theology. For your entire Christian life, you will be engaged in an ongoing process of examining your beliefs and comparing them with the Scriptures. This book will help in that process. At times you will appreciate the new truths you will learn. At other times you will question them. But you will always be challenged to make the Bible your guide and to bring your thinking to the Word of God for approval.

A "New" Notion of Personal Responsibility

I have many books in my library on the subject of marriage. I have perused hundreds of other volumes over the years in libraries and bookstores. Almost without exception they have the same approach. They stress the right of readers to be happy and instruct them how to find that happiness. While it is true that God desires that you have an abundant life, His method is drastically different from that of the world. He starts from the premise that your personal responsibilities are more important than your "rights." As someone once said, "The teaching of rights breeds rebellion. The teaching of responsibilities brings revival." Many couples spend a lifetime fixated on their rights, and they set out to make their mate meet their demands. They learn to see their mate as the major problem in the marriage and set out to change them. They fail to see their own responsibility, let alone work on fulfilling it.

In the pages ahead you will find yourself challenged to focus on your own responsibilities rather than your partner's. This may be a radical departure from what you have tried before. But I ask you what I once asked a man who was on the very verge of divorce.

He prided himself on "telling it like it is" and holding nothing back. When he felt it, he said it. I asked, "And how is that working for you?" How is your natural way of doing things working for you in your marriage? Maybe you need a radical departure from what comes natural. I can assure you that what comes natural is not supernatural.

Tried and Proven Concepts

This book is not about theory. It is a compilation of truths and concepts discovered through years of biblical research and tested through thousands of hours of marriage counseling spanning almost four decades. The couples who have come to me for help have already tried all the worn-out spiritual clichés. They are wearied by the flippant advice given by well-meaning friends. They are tired of faddish theories of pop psychology. They want answers!

I have been forced to my knees many times after catching the tears of the brokenhearted. Much of what I have learned is revealed in the pages of this book. Uncovered in the mine of God's Word and tested in the laboratory of human suffering, these principles work!

An Emphasis on "Ministry"

A friend once asked me about this book. "What's with the title? Why call it *The Ministry of Marriage?* Isn't that a bit unusual?" It is unusual to apply the word "ministry" to the relationship of marriage. Usually, marriage is presented in a variety of other ways suggesting that it is merely an extension of dating bliss into wedded bliss, a perpetual romance of soft candlelight and flowers, or a haven from all cares. Such concepts reflect the notion that marriage means happiness and warm feelings that are effortlessly received. Believing this results in expectations of passive enjoyment from which demands for pleasure become the battle cry.

The Bible, on the other hand, brings a needed balance to the discussion about matrimony. It does not deny warm feelings, but it shows them as the fruit of obedience rather than the responsibility of your mate. Its emphasis is on ministry.

Christ is the model of all we are to do and be in this life. *"As he is, so are we in this world"* (I John 4:17); therefore, since He *"came not to be ministered unto, but to minister"* (Matt. 20:28), so should we. This quality of our Lord is one you will see often in your reading, and the need of following His example to minister is a consistent refrain as well. That's because bringing this commitment to marriage is a step toward Christlikeness, and Christlikeness is the beginning of genuine joy.

A Counselor's Heart

There is great value in a marriage counselor writing a book on marriage. After listening to the needs of hundreds of couples, you begin to understand what the common struggles really are. It becomes obvious that there are similar issues faced by all, and that there are answers for them. Contrary to what most couples believe, there are no "new" problems in marriage; they are all "common to man."

I do not claim to be an "expert" (defined: "ex" as "has been," and "spert" as "a small drip under pressure"), but I have been down a road that many have never traveled. First, I have been married for thirty-six years to a wonderful girl and during that time we have experienced the growth of our love and devotion to one another. We have had some struggles but have grown through them. The love we have now is uniquely different from when we first married. That original love has not been replaced, but so much has been added to it. Because we have experienced marital disappointments that are common to other marriages, I can offer the comfort with which God has comforted us (II Cor. 1:3-5).

Second, as I have caught the tears of many husbands and many wives, I have learned that God has the answer for troubled marriages. There was a time when I would rush to the psychology texts for answers. Then I learned to go to God's Word. Now I go to God's Word and to my knees. God is indeed the Wonderful Counselor.

Third, I have learned to speak the truth in love (Eph. 4:15). It is this balance of truth and love that I have attempted to achieve in this book. I will tell you the truth. Sometimes you will like it (especially when you agree), and sometimes you won't, but my goal is to give the truth of God's Word. At the same time, I attempt to balance it in love.

IRONCLAD GUARANTEES FOR THIS BOOK

Everyone likes guarantees, especially the "money back" kind. While I cannot offer a "money back guarantee," I can offer at least two guarantees that you can take to the bank.

First, the truths you are about to learn will cause you pain. As you read some of these pages, you may want to fasten your seat belt, don your safety helmet, and call the insurance company.

Truth causes pain because it may take you out of your comfort zone of thinking and living. You have probably acquired a style of cohabiting with your mate that comes very naturally to you. Over the years, your way of living has become a very dear friend, one who understands and makes no demands upon you. You are comfortable with this friend because he tells you only what you want to hear. Now, you may learn some things contrary to his advice. This may exert pressure on you to leave the "flowery beds of ease" and take up the cross of sacrifice, of ministry, and of death to self. This can be a painful experience.

Some couples are not willing to pay the price. They deal with pain on the front end of marriage by seeking guarantees of safety. They enter a trial marriage hoping to test their compatibility before tying the knot. Such couples who live together before marriage are 80 percent more likely to divorce than those who do not. Others sign a prenuptial contract or opt merely to live together without any intention of marrying. If the pain can't be avoided on the front end, many seek to find relief in the midst of it. They decide to divorce. Such fearful souls have never learned that there is a price to pay for a spiritual, committed relationship. One such price is the painfulness of learning the very truth that offers hope.

It is not by accident that God's Word alludes to the effects of truth as a "wound": *"Faithful are the wounds of a friend"* (Prov. 27:6). Sometimes we are called upon to comfort the afflicted, at other times to afflict the comfortable. I hope, if you are afflicted, you will find comfort. But if you are comfortable, you may feel afflicted. After all, the use of a metaphor of a "two-edged sword" to describe the Scripture with the effect of *"piercing,"* even *"dividing asunder of soul and spirit"* (Heb 4:12), does not exactly communicate visions of comfort.

The second guarantee is that there will be no rapid and dramatic change in your marriage. As much as I would like to make a better offer, there is no quick fix for relationship stress. It takes time to create a problem and it takes time to correct it. Frustrated indeed is the couple who has fought bitterly for twenty years and expects that one visit to a counselor or a cursory reading of a single book will undo all the damage. At least forty days (approximately six weeks) are required to effect a long-time change. And that is forty days of focused effort, earnest prayer, and intense study.

This is something that many do not realize about spiritual growth. They want "instant sanctification." They expect that a trip to the altar, a few tears, and a sincere emotion or two will suffice, but they are wrong. The trip to the altar is good, the tears are good, and if there are sincere feelings, they are good too. But that is just the beginning. Once a decision is made, it will require the consistent application of new truth and changed behavior over a period of time for the new way of thinking and acting to become as habitual and natural as the old.

For that reason, I recommend that you follow your initial reading of this book with a chapter by chapter study. You may want to take notes as you read, meditate on the various Scripture references cited, and even discuss your findings with your mate. You may use the book for your devotions together, reading aloud to one another and praying together. If a particular Bible text impresses you, consider memorizing it so that you can mull it over while you drive or work around the house. These truths will make an excellent resource for a Sunday school emphasis or a series of sermons. Anything you can do to impress these precepts into your heart and mind for a protracted period of time will be helpful for assimilation into your life and marriage. Just be prepared to go the distance.

This book should be seen then, as a starting place for change, a jump-start for the marathon run, but it is a beginning.

Hope

Above all, this book represents hope! If the source of hope is the *"God of hope"* (Rom. 15:13), if you through the *"comfort of the Scriptures might have hope"* (Rom. 15:4), and if you *"abound in hope, through the power of the Holy Ghost"* (Rom. 15:13), then you are starting on a journey of rich discoveries of hope! For here, in these pages, you will find God on every page, scriptural principles, and an appeal to rely upon the Holy Spirit to help you to understand and apply them.

In fact, you will begin that journey on the next page.

1

THERE IS HOPE FOR YOUR MARRIAGE!

A friend recently confided in me, "Brother Jim, I have lost all hope for my marriage." I can vividly recall the emptiness of his downcast eyes and the hollowness of his words. His head was slung low and his shoulders slumped in abject despair. My heart was gripped by the poignancy of his sorrow. I thought, "How tragic when a man loses hope!"

How does a man get to a place of such forlorn sorrow? What causes such hopelessness? What happens in a marriage to cause such defeat? This man began his marriage with all the idealism of youthful love and joined a young bride at the wedding altar with the greatest of dreams for the future. They had basked in the soft glow of the unity candle. How did the light fade? Why did the dreams vanish? Where did the idealism go?

Because marriage is so intimate, so spiritual, and uniquely complex, it harbors many causes of hopelessness. One cause may be the chronic friction of personality differences. While it is true that "opposites attract," the very differences that initially attract a couple to one another can be the things that eventually drive them apart. I once knew a woman who was bubbly and vivacious and loved to talk. She met a strong, silent man. This was perfect! She had someone to talk to who would sit quietly and listen to her for hours. He, on the other hand, was happy that he didn't have to do any talking at all. Twenty-five years passed and they came for counseling. "He never talks!" she complained. "He just sits there and never says a word. I never know what he's thinking or how he's feeling."

"She won't shut up!" the husband interjected. "She talks about anything and everything! There's never a moment of peace." The very thing that had drawn them together now threatened to destroy their marriage.

Another cause of hopelessness is the waning of emotional love. Most couples are shocked to find that the initial euphoria of romantic love can take a beating over time. They watched it happen to their parents and had even observed it in other seasoned marriages but swore in their youthful idealism that it would never happen to them. But it did, and for good reason: *"because iniquity shall abound, the love of many shall wax cold"* (Matt. 24:12). Man's sinful nature and the debilitating nature of the flesh guarantee a constant drain on the best of relationships.

Other causes include financial pressures, in-law problems, and differences in parenting styles. Add to these the ever-present tension of sexual adjustment and communication breakdowns, and the picture is clearer. When the less obvious but powerfully influential causes such as spiritual coldness and even spiritual warfare are factored in, the focus becomes clearer still.

Whatever the reasons, many couples lose hope for their future. In over thirty years of marriage counseling, I have seen this happen in countless relationships. Here at the Moorehead Manor, hundreds of people have come for counseling, most for their marriages. Almost without exception, they have lost a grip on hope. One distraught wife typifies the fear of many: "Is there any hope for our marriage?" she asked pleadingly. Perhaps you are like her. Maybe you've even harbored the same question in your own heart. If so, you are not alone. *"There hath no temptation taken you but such as is common to man"* (I Cor. 10:13). This commonality of life's struggles is underscored by Christ in a gripping summation of His earthly ministry. He stood before a hometown crowd in Nazareth and preached from Isaiah 61:1–2:

"The Spirit of the Lord is upon me, because he hath anointed me to preach the gospel to the poor; he hath sent me to heal the brokenhearted, to preach deliverance to the captives, and recovering of sight to the blind,

to set at liberty them that are bruised, to preach the acceptable year of the Lord" (Luke 4:18–19).

In a concise yet sweeping statement, our Lord describes the common burdens of mankind. These burdens that plague man also affect relationships. What is common to man is also common to marriages.

The "Poor" Marriage

The poor marriage is the marriage that is impoverished; it is *"poor in spirit."* This is a marriage that is struggling because of a lack of hope. You may be in a marriage characterized by a sense of spiritual helplessness. You were once full of hope and full of faith, but your resources have been so drained that you see little light ahead. You long ago ceased being conscious of the power of faith and have settled into the habit of being conscious of the problem. Fear has displaced faith. While you once had great faith in God to direct your future and preserve your union, you may feel that your faith was misplaced because it seems that God has not come through for you. While your devotion was once the "tie that binds," it now seems that duty is the tie. These are indicators of a depletion of hope. You are indeed poor in spirit. Such hopelessness is common to man and common to marriages. But Christ came to *"preach the gospel* [good news]*"* for you. There is hope!

I often open a week of counseling with words of encouragement to couples. I tell them, "Even if your faith is weak and your hope is low, it's okay. You can lean on mine if you have to. My faith is strong and my hope is high! I have seen God do too much in hurting marriages to doubt that He can do it for you as well! The time may come when I have to lean on yours, but for now you can lean on mine."

It is a good thing, is it not, that we can *"bear one another's burdens"*? But far better than this is the fact that you can lean on Christ's faith. As He prayed for Peter that his *"faith fail not"* (Luke 22:32), He prayed for you as well. That's right. Before you were married, and even before you were born, He prayed for you. After praying for His disciples, Christ continued, *"Neither pray I for these alone, but for them also which shall believe on me through their word"* (John 17:20). He was looking ahead, down through the future to the time you and your mate would believe on Him; and He prayed specifically that your two hearts might be one: *"that they may be one, even as we are one"* (v. 22). Just as the Son and the Father are one, Christ prayed that you and your mate would be one.

How does one describe the mystical spiritual union of the Father and the Son? They are two separate entities yet marvelously united and inseparable. This merging of persons is a mystery indeed. But even though he cannot fully comprehend it, he can revel in the knowledge that Christ prayed that a Christian marriage might enjoy the same closeness as the oneness of the Father-Son relationship.

I can hear the skeptic's response, "Yeah, right. If that's true, then why hasn't there been a change in my marriage?" The delay may be traceable to several reasons. First, God's answer may be delayed by demonic interference. In Daniel 10, Daniel prayed and a heavenly messenger brought an answer to him. But Satan delayed this messenger for three full weeks! In the meantime, Daniel went through some real spiritual agony. He persevered, however, and ultimately saw the answer.

A lack of change in the marriage may be because of sinful resistance to the will of God. In some cases, the answer is obvious but is refused. A Bible example is the refusal of the Hebrews to enter into the Promised Land. Instead they chose to believe the lies of the faithless spies and lost the blessing intended for them (Num. 13–14). The blessings that God intends for some marriages are never enjoyed because they are never claimed. The Promised Land is out there, but you must first believe that God is greater than the giants and that the grapes of Eshcol are better fare than campfire cooking.

The delay of reprieve can be traceable to a belief system rooted in the *"tradition of men, after the rudiments of the world, and not after Christ"* (Col. 2:8). Men and the world offer much advice and many options that are not spiritual. Such things spoil, or literally bind up, the believer. Advice such as "it's okay to be angry," or "it's all your mate's fault," or even "you just need to walk away from this and get a fresh start" are not from God but from men and the world.

If you have been wondering where your relief is and when the answer will arrive, and you have begun to question God, your lack of relief may have more to do with your sense of timing than His. There are two elements to the completed will of God: direction and timing. Equating the two is foolish, if not dangerous, and is certainly frustrating. Until there is a marriage of God's direction and timing, His will is not complete. A young couple is in love and has determined that it's God's will for them to marry. They assume that because they're getting married anyway, why not now! They are sixteen years old, have yet to graduate from high school, have no job and no marketable skills, but they insist that it's God's will. They have made the mistake of equating God's direction and God's timing.

Marital harmony is obviously God's direction for every couple, but that is not to say it will automatically come in the way and the time that they envision. My wife Sandra and I have been happily married for twenty-seven years. (We've been married over thirty-five years.) I'm being facetious, of course, to illustrate a point; in God's will and timing, it took a while for a certain unnamed husband (thick-headed clod that he is) to yield to Him. His direction was there all along, but God knew that He needed time to prepare me for the marital blessings I now enjoy.

Yes, Christ has prayed for your union, and despite your frustration with the delay, He keeps on praying. He even now lives to make intercession for you in your poverty, your time of need. It is not your faith that is as important as His faith, and His faith is abundant for you. There is hope.

THE "BROKENHEARTED" MARRIAGE

The brokenhearted marriage is one of chronic discouragement, despair, and depression. You may have come to the point of fatalism, thinking that misery and unhappiness are your unavoidable destiny. It is not uncommon at the Manor for us to host couples whose goal in counseling is to determine whether they really want to stay in their marriage.

As I greeted one new arrival, his first words to me were, "If this week doesn't work, we're getting a divorce!" They had lost hope. But as I prayed for them and exposed their thirsty souls to the living water of Christ, an amazing transformation took place. After the first session, when they turned their backs on one another and spat angry words, I witnessed a softening of the hard edges. On the fourth day of counseling, I looked out the window to see them actually walking down the lane together. It was the fall of the year and the sun's rays magnified the brightness of the reddish orange maple trees. The lane was overarched with the branches forming a cathedral of light backlighted by an azure sky. As they walked, she reached out to take his hand. He pushed it away and put his arm around her. She laid her head on his shoulder, and I cried. I was witnessing the healing of the brokenhearted.

A wife once confessed to me that she felt that her marriage was God's punishment for her youthful promiscuity. It is not surprising that she struggled with chronic debilitating depression. Hers was truly a brokenhearted union.

It is not unusual for couples to request separate rooms when they come to the Manor. Because we encourage a practice that I euphemistically call "proximity therapy," we disallow this with rare exceptions. One of these exceptions occurred when we counseled a divorced couple. Since they weren't legally married, I allowed them to have individual rooms. Again God moved in, and after a couple of days He began thawing the iciness between them. Then one night, after working late, I was walking through the darkened house past the laundry room. I detected some movement and saw them silhouetted against a moonlit window . . . and they were making out! They had left their rooms to rendezvous in the laundry room. Now I was in a quandary; should I send them to their rooms? Reprimand them? Give them a demerit? Then I remembered, this is why they're here! This is what we've been praying for!

It is to such marriages that Christ came with a compassionate goal *"to heal the brokenhearted,"* and He will do that for you. There is hope!

The "Captive" Marriage

A captive is a person who is bound by sin. A captive marriage includes those individuals caught in the grip of sinful habits, lustful perversions, and self-gratification. More and more I counsel couples whose marriages have been nearly destroyed by all manner of immorality. Our wonderful Lord came to bring deliverance from such bondage, and He can do it for you.

A dear hurting couple came after the husband's sin had been uncovered. His chronic adulteries had only recently been exposed and the marriage was on the verge of divorce. He broke before God and repented of his sins. God poured the balm of healing over a terrible wound with miraculous results. Eight years later this couple came to hear me preach. Over dinner, the wife took her husband's hand and, with tears of joy, said, "We have never been so in love. We feel like a couple of teenagers who are dating!" God really can set the captive free. There is hope!

The "Blind" Marriage

Blindness has always carried a connotation of darkness and lostness. Spiritual blindness is worse than physical blindness in many ways. Helen Keller was once asked if she could think of anything worse than being blind. "Yes," she replied, "having sight but no vision." When the vision of a married couple is lost, it is a terrible thing. They have lost sight of God's power to save.

Elisha the prophet was trapped by a vast enemy army at Dothan (II Kings 6). His servant discovered their plight on an early morning walk. He took one look at the multitudes of horses and chariots and cried out, *"Alas my master! how shall we do?"* Elisha saw what the servant could not. *"Fear not,"* he said, *"for they that be with us are more than they that be with them."* He saw help where the servant saw only helplessness. God in His goodness seems always to have someone with vision for those with none, visionaries who have a burden for the blind to see. Elisha prayed for his fearful servant, *"Lord, I pray thee, open his eyes, that he may see."* His prayer was answered with miraculous results: *"And the Lord opened the eyes of the young man; and he saw; and, behold, the mountain was full of horses and chariots of fire round about Elisha"* (v. 17). The heavenly host far outnumbered the earthly enemy and had all along! The servant though was blinded to his deliverance until God opened his eyes.

God's will for the blind is their *"recovering of sight."* He will open your eyes. Help is available. The mountains are full of it! God wants you to *"lift up [your] eyes unto the hills from whence cometh [your] help"* (Ps. 121:1). Blindness is not a permanent condition. A renewed vision is just a prayer away. There is hope!

THE "BRUISED" MARRIAGE

The bruised are those who have been beaten down so persistently that they feel there is no relief. It is the result of perpetual strife. A marriage in this state is one in which the struggles are long-term and seemingly so irresolvable that hope has slowly died. One blow to the body may not bruise it, but perpetual blows to the same area not only bruise but with each blow drive the wound deeper into the flesh.

As a child I encountered a schoolyard bully who delighted in demonstrating his physical supremacy to anyone foolish enough to challenge him. I had no sooner done so when he grabbed me in a headlock and told me that I had to cry "Uncle" before he would release me. Determined that I could break free, and too stubborn and prideful to give up, I fought to free myself. He only tightened his grip and dug his bony arm deeper into my neck. I could feel the burning sensation of a growing friction rash, and as he persisted in his diabolical punishment, the pain deepened. What started as a rash had now become a bruise. I needed deliverance.

The woman with the issue of blood in Luke 8 had endured her condition for twelve long years and had spent all her money on doctors to no avail. She had only to touch the hem of the Great Physician's garment to find healing. Like countless people who appeal to Christ for deliverance, she found it.

Numerous people have come to the Manor who have been labeled with some permanent "disorder," having spent thousands of dollars on therapy and medication without experiencing any change. Some have even been locked away in mental institutions. We have seen them find deliverance in Christ.

I recall a case in which countless hours of therapy had had little effect. In desperation, this couple came to me. I observed their anger and their bitter words, then announced, "I know what the problem is." They were incredulous. "You know what the problem is? We have spent a fortune on medication, been to the top psychiatrists who told us there was no hope, and you can tell already what the problem is?" "Yes," I replied. "I would like for you to read a Scripture aloud." And I asked them to open their Bibles to Proverbs 13:10: *"Only by pride cometh contention: but with the well advised is wisdom."* God opened their eyes and they experienced reconciliation and found hope for the future. Why? By translating psychological diagnoses into plain Bible terms, they found hope. "Pride" has a biblical answer, but "Avoidant Personality Disorder," "Social Anxiety Disorder," "Impulse Control Disorder," and so forth elude a cure. Instead the only hope offered is the hope to cope via ongoing therapy and mind-altering drugs. This couple could now enjoy a biblical diagnosis and along with it a biblical cure.

Psychology with its 250 various systems of approach and its 10,000 varying techniques is strong at describing the problem. The *Diagnostic Statistical Manual* (DSM) of the American Psychiatric Association offers 400 plus labels, disorders, and categories of human problems. Most of them have multiple subheadings and many detailed descriptions. Because of this, it appears that the DSM is authoritative and even scientific. While appearing strong at describing problems, psychology is weak in explaining them and unable to cure them. Biblical counseling on the other hand is strong at explaining problems and expert at the cure.

This couple had allowed secular therapists to define their condition, arbitrarily label them with various disorders, and control their regimen of therapy. This resulted in their being distracted from spiritual hope in a biblical solution. (Apparently, some well-meaning but misguided psychologists have a "Messianic Pseudo-Scientific Labeling Disorder.") I simply allowed the Word of God, which *is a discerner of the thoughts and intents of the heart"* (Heb. 4:12), to do its work. And it does! When Christian couples stop justifying their sin by the language of the world and begin judging their sin by the language of the Word, healing can begin.

Many marriages with chronic struggles and long-term failure have experienced a similar crisis. Although they may not have been labeled by a psychologist, they may have been condemned by the "accuser" or convinced by their own wounded spirit that hope is elusive. But like the woman with the issue of blood, they need only a touch of the Great Physician's hem to find healing and deliverance.

When Christ addressed the needs of the poor, the brokenhearted, and the captives, He was illustrating how common these problems are. When He included the blind and the bruised, He widened the circle to encompass all of humanity to illustrate that these struggles are common.

A big question on the minds of many is "Am I normal?" It is reassuring to know that others understand and that they have experienced what you are going through. Let me assure you, you are normal. What you are experiencing is *"common to man."* I know the lure of thinking you are somehow unique, that nobody in the world can possibly understand your sufferings, that no one else has suffered like you. But be assured, dear friend, that there are thousands just like you, going through the same valley and the same struggles. It seems painfully lonely, this path on which you find yourself. As you fix your gaze on the horizon, you see nobody. As you look behind you, you cannot find another soul traveling with you. But if you look down, you will notice countless footprints, the tracks of numberless pilgrims who have gone this way before.

More importantly, if your temptation is *"common to man,"* the Lord Jesus Christ has also experienced the same temptation. He was *"in all points tempted like as we are."* In His humanity, He willingly entered into your struggles: *"Wherefore in all things it behoved him to be made like unto his brethren, that he might be a merciful and faithful high priest. . . . For in that he himself hath suffered being tempted, he is able to succour them that are tempted"* (Heb. 2:17–18). As a result, He is *"touched with the feeling of [your] infirmities"* and the Scriptures exhort us to *"therefore come boldly unto the throne of grace, that we may obtain mercy, and find grace to help in time of need"* (Heb. 4:15–16). Because Christ has faced our temptation before us, He has conquered death and sin, and we have *"Christ in you, the hope of glory"* (Col. 1:27), then *"we are more than conquerors through him that loved us"* (Rom. 8:37).

After preaching a series of messages on marriage at an isolated country retreat, I was approached by a true mountain man (and a mountain of a man). Dressed in bib overalls and a T-shirt, he sported a well-worn baseball cap and a two- or three-day growth of stubble on his chin and face. The most noticeable thing about him, however, was the wad of chewing tobacco, which caused one cheek to bulge and produced a small dark rivulet of tobacco juice out of one corner of his mouth. "Revurn," he began, "I like yur talks n' all, but I got one probum with whatcha bin sayin'." He punctuated this sentence by spitting an impressive amount of tobacco juice at my feet and applying a sweep of his hand to wipe the lingering effects from his chin. "I bin married forty-four yure," he said. (I was distracted by the movement of the bulge and a nervous fear of getting in the path of the next offering.) "And if thur's one thang I've lurn'd," (Splat! Another deposit at my feet) "it is that yew caint revive what ain't alive." Splat!

I was disappointed that he held this view even after eight sessions of hope-building preaching on God's power to revive a marriage. Furthermore, having never enjoyed such a colorful review of my preaching, I was at first somewhat distracted in my response. But once I collected my thoughts, I replied, "That's an interesting thought, but Lazarus would probably disagree! As would Jairus's daughter, the widow's son, and even the Lord Jesus Christ Himself! In fact," I continued, "it is the specialty of our Lord to do that very thing! He *majors* in reviving what ain't alive."

This man had given in to the common temptation of questioning the power of God to deliver from a disappointing marriage by virtue of his own painful experiences and the frustration of being in a marital rut. A country preacher once defined "rut" to me as "a grave with both ends kicked out." When a person lives in such a grave for "forty-four yure," it can be discouraging indeed.

The ingredients of marriages in such a rut are many and varied: they include poverty of spirit, brokenheartedness in relationships, bondage to sin, blindness of vision, and a wounded and bruised spirit. But our wonderful Lord overcomes each one with tender care and loving attention to detail. Is your marriage poor? He preaches "good news" to it. Is it brokenhearted? He wants to heal it. Is it captive? Then He offers deliverance. Is it blind? He will help it recover its sight. Is your marriage bruised? Christ will set it at liberty.

Our God provides a power that guarantees perpetual hope! It is the *"exceeding greatness of his power to us-ward who believe, according to the working of his mighty power, which he wrought in Christ, when he raised him from the dead"* (Eph. 1:19–20).

The same power that raised our Lord from the dead is at work in your marriage! What God did in Christ, He will do in you.

God *can* revive what ain't alive. There *is* hope!

---

[1] Lloyd Ogilvie, A Future and a Hope (Word, 1998), 74.

2

The Biblical Path to Marital Victory

But God be thanked, that ye were the servants of sin,
but ye have obeyed from the heart that form of doctrine
which was delivered you.
Romans 6:17

One of the greatest causes of marital failure is unfulfilled expectations: *"Hope deferred maketh the heart sick"* (Prov. 13:12). The hope referred to here is an expectation of good or an idealized goal. When such an ideal or goal is deferred ("terminated" or "delayed"), the heart gets "sick." This is a Bible term for depression.

When someone's child fails to meet his expectation as a parent, he may experience discouragement or even depression. When one loses his job, a loved one dies, or an anticipated promotion fails to materialize, the heart is affected. In each case, because an expectation is not realized, depression sets in.

The idealistic couple rarely pauses long enough before the wedding to consider the downside of matrimony. In fact, they not only fail to see any benefit of doing this but also resent any attempts of marital veterans to point out the downside. They don't understand the value of counting the costs before building a tower. One reason for this is their optimistic certainty that their marriage will be different from those before them. Fully 96 percent of youth will marry, and 78 percent of them emphatically declare that divorce will never happen!

Another reason for not entertaining any negative information about the coming nuptials is that most couples build their expectation about marriage from idealistic notions: fairy tales (remember "and they lived happily ever after"?), romance novels, romantic movies, and love songs. They are experienced practitioners of relationship love gleaned from numerous dating experiences and have assumed that the only reason the feelings didn't last for their previous lovers was that they weren't really the right one. But now that they have found "Mr. or Miss Right," they are absolutely certain that love can grow only stronger when they are thrust into intimate proximity to the object of their love. They have a "hope" for their marriage.

Now hope is a good thing if it comes from the right source. When expectations are grounded in spiritual sources, they always come through. David encouraged us to *"hope thou in God"* (Ps. 42), perhaps because he himself had learned to: *"My soul, wait thou only upon God; for my expectation is from him"* (Ps. 62:5). He had learned the invaluable lesson of basing his expectations squarely upon his God alone.

This alignment of expectations is a great value of premarital counseling. The degree of satisfaction in marriage is directly proportionate to the quality of preparation before marriage. A study of 4,500 married Air Force Academy graduates over a multi-year period revealed some astounding results. The divorce rate was only .004 percent![1] Compared to the typical divorce rate of approximately 50 percent of new marriages in the general population, this news provided a stark contrast. How was this possible? The answer is surprisingly simple. After graduation, engaged couples were enrolled in a fourteen-session course on marriage. Doctors, lawyers, financial counselors, and pastors taught the classes. Many potential areas of trouble were targeted and much frothy enthusiasm was replaced with hard reality. The young couples were warned about potential danger areas and then equipped with information on how to deal with them.

I have counseled many Christian couples over the last quarter of a century and have found that few of them have had any preparation at all. This may be in part because only 35 percent of pastors nationwide require premarital counseling, even though over 90 percent of youth desire it.

I have informally surveyed over four thousand Christian marriage partners in my marriage conferences and found that only 5 percent of them have had any preparation at all. In one meeting with two hundred married adults present, not one had received any counseling or teaching on marriage whatsoever before tying the knot. Even a dogcatcher is required to have more training than that!

When false expectations are not addressed before the wedding, serious problems can develop afterwards. One of these, according to Richard Exley, is that of expanding one's expectations: "It is but a small step from expectation to demand, and from demand to abuse."[2] It is no secret that one of the common expectations of youthful love is that "marriage will make me happy and fulfilled." Happiness and fulfillment have been the standard fare of a couple's relationship with one another before marriage, and they assume that such will continue after marriage. In fact, some believe it will not merely continue but get better and better! Such expansive expectations can easily harden into a selfish mindset, which ultimately demands satisfaction. Like a spoiled child who is accustomed to getting whatever he desires, an adult who has pampered himself with unrestrained emotional gratification before marriage comes to believe it is his right to have it afterwards.

Ideally, these goals should be addressed during engagement or even before, but whether they were or not, they can be corrected afterwards. One of the strengths of the Christian faith is that present conformity to Christ is not due to one's past but in spite of it. In a powerful treatise on the power of people to change, the apostle Paul writes to the pagan Romans who had successfully overcome a licentious past: *"God be thanked, that ye were the [slaves] of sin, but ye have obeyed from the heart that form of doctrine which was delivered you"* (Rom. 6:17).

As you read this, you may be skeptical and unbelieving because you really don't believe that your marriage can change. You have often tried to change but have been disappointed so often that you have begun to wonder if it's possible at all. If there is one thing I hope to impart to you, it is that change is possible!

I grew up on a farm. When I attended a county fair for the first time, I was unaccustomed to such extravaganzas and was absolutely agog at the sights and the sounds of it all. Imagine my thrill at my first glimpse of a live elephant. He was a behemoth of a monster towering over his handler and as big as a corn shed! I was puzzled however to see that his only restraint was a thin rope tied to a stake in the ground. He could have walked off with the stake if he'd had a mind to. He could have walked off with the entire fair if he had a mind to! That was just it; he didn't have a mind to, and with good reason. As a small calf, he had been tied to a tree stump with a logging chain around his leg. The first time he attempted to escape, he ran full speed and was unceremoniously dumped on his belly when he reached the end of the chain. He bawled a bit, backed up, and tried again, only to be dumped again. He repeated this process several times until his little pea brain concluded that resistance on the leg equaled impossible escape. Thereafter, his handlers needed only to use the lightest weight line and a small stake. The elephant had been conditioned for captivity.

Like the baby elephant, many marriages are also conditioned to captivity. They have failed and tried to make it right. Then they failed again. Each time they failed, they were conditioned to believe that there was less hope than before. Eventually, they gave in to a mindset of defeatism and despair. Because divorce was not an option, and neither was fulfillment, they chose a cold war. The home became a house, a demilitarized zone where miserable coexistence became a way of life.

I once knew a couple who could not get along with one another. They refused to divorce because of religious convictions but could find no joy in their marriage. They finally agreed to a truce of sorts. He moved into a separate bedroom in a remote corner of the house, and they agreed to never see or speak to one another. There were two notable exceptions—Christmas and Thanksgiving dinner. They did this for the sake of the children. What a cheerless reunion that must have been! They were married, even living under the same roof, but they were divorced. They weren't divorced geographically because they lived together; they were divorced emotionally. Sadly, many couples share such a disheartening arrangement. They don't always formalize an agreement like my friends, but they have one nonetheless.

This doesn't have to be! You can *"do all things through Christ which strengtheneth [you]"* (Phil. 4:13). The Devil may seem to have the upper hand, but *"greater is he that is in you, than he that is in the world"* (I John 4:4). Defeat is not an option because *"this is the victory that overcometh the world, even our faith"* (I John 5:4). You *can* change. Your marriage can change. Your future can change.

THE TIMING OF VICTORY

Victory will take time no doubt, but it can happen. Don't make the mistake of assuming a short change for a long problem. Life habits require time to heal and relationship ruts are not filled in overnight. Jay Adams estimates that lasting change requires at least forty days, or approximately six weeks.[3] A tearful trip to the altar or a teeth-grinding resolve is not enough. It may be a beginning but it's not enough. Once you make a decision to apply truth to your marriage, it will mean at least forty days of prayer, effort, and thought in applying the truth before the truth replaces the lie and the new way of thinking and acting becomes as habitual as the old. That's at least forty days. In some cases, it may take longer.

We live in an age of the instant. Every problem on TV is resolved within an hour. Every question can be answered on the Internet in seconds. We are an impatient people wanting everything now. There is no powder mix for happy marriages. It is not a matter of adding water and stirring. It takes time. Many people don't understand the need of time.

Spiritual growth, whether in your personal life or in relationships, isn't quick or easy. There are no buttons to push or levers to pull that will guarantee a change. There is no panacea pill to pop, no mantra to recite, no effortless fairy tale solution.

While spiritual growth may not be quick or easy, it is certain. It will happen because it's in God's plan for you: *"I know the thoughts that I think toward you, saith the Lord, thoughts of peace, and not of evil, to give you an expected end"* (Jer. 29:11). God has you in His thoughts and on His heart. He thinks ahead to the goal He desires for you, an expected end. He is in control and you can trust Him. When He sovereignly arranged your marriage, He had every intention of making it prosper: *"Being confident of this very thing, that he which hath begun a good work in you will perform it until the day of Jesus Christ"* (Phil. 1:6). Our God finishes what He starts.

He is the source of all victory that you desire. The question is, do you see God as the *only* source of *all* your help? If you don't, you will feel overwhelmed and defeated from the outset. I experienced this feeling as a young pastor. I had assumed the pastorate of a church twice as big as the one I had just left. I remember walking into the new auditorium and thinking, "How can I ever lead such a church? I am so weak and incapable." I was beginning to sink in a mire of depressing, defeatist thoughts when I was struck with the recollection of an unfamiliar Scripture. I had to look it up in a concordance to assure myself that it was in fact in the Bible: *"Faithful is he that calleth you, who also will do it"* (I Thess. 5:24). How my heart was encouraged when I focused my thoughts on God's power instead of my frailty.

The Source of Victory

When Paul wrote, *"God be thanked,"* he didn't say "your methods be thanked," "your inner child be thanked," or "your therapist be thanked." He said, "God be thanked." He didn't say "my preaching be thanked," "my counseling be thanked," or "the church be thanked." He said, "God be thanked." Every counselor needs to return to this truth. Every psychologist and psychiatrist needs to face this reality. Every seeker of truth needs to bow before this fact. It is not a theory, technique, methodology, or philosophy that changes people; it is God and God alone! *"For it is God which worketh in you both to will and to do of his good pleasure"* (Phil. 2:13). It is God and God alone who can change the heart of a human being: *"The king's heart is in the hand of the Lord, as the rivers of water: he turneth it whithersoever he will"* (Prov. 21:1).

Paul was amazed that some lose sight of their initial focus. *"I marvel that ye are so soon removed from him that called you into the grace of Christ unto another gospel"* (Gal. 1:6). He challenged his converts to remember that the source of lasting victory is the same as the source for initial victory: *"Being confident of this very thing, that he which hath begun a good work in you will perform it until the day of Jesus Christ"* (Phil. 1:6). He questioned their wisdom in beginning well with Christ, then attempting to continue well without Him: *"Are ye so foolish? having begun in the Spirit, are ye now made perfect by the flesh?"* (Gal. 3:3).

Spiritual leaders share his bewilderment. Why do so many people find hope and help in the church for salvation and then look outside the church for ultimate change? Why do they welcome the Word of God for the truth needed to turn from sin but look to man's wisdom in psychology to keep from sinning? Why do they see the church pastor as wise enough to lead the lost from sin but not wise enough to help them live above sin? What does it say about our focus when we begin the Christian life in the Spirit and seek to continue in the flesh? Are modern Christians so sophisticated that we have outgrown the simplicity of Christ?

Where are you looking for help, dear reader? If it is in anything or anyone but God, you will be disappointed. On the other hand, everything you desire is found in Him. What do you need? Acceptance? You are *"accepted in the beloved"* (Eph. 1:6). Completeness? You are *"complete in* him" (Col. 2:10). Sufficiency? *"Our sufficiency is of God"* (II Cor. 3:5) Despite the teaching of the world, Christ really is all you need.

I fear that oftentimes the ruler of the darkness roams freely through the corridors of our hearts. He seems to be solely in control of our fate. We appear alone and helpless before his advances. We look at our feeble resources and conclude, *"with men this is impossible,"* but then we remember, *"with God all things are possible"* (Matt. 19:26). You may feel all alone as you whisper by rote "just me and Jesus" at the sound of the intruder, but remember that sitting nearby and poised to strike is the Lion of the Tribe of Judah, and He is the all-powerful one.

Paul exults in the power of God to change man at the deepest level. In giving Him thanks for the obedience of the Roman believers, Paul is glorifying God's power, not man's resolve. That's why he said, "God be thanked."

The Method of Victory

Paul identifies the three parts of man that God changes—the intellect, the heart, and the will.

The intellect, or the mind, is that which is alluded to with the word "doctrine." Doctrine, or teaching, is addressed to the mind. Unfortunately, the minds of many are blinded by Satan, are distracted by the allurements of worldly philosophies, and are seemingly beyond the reach of man's grasp. Paul writes that man can actually be mentally opposed to God: you . . . were . . . *alienated and enemies in your mind"* (Col. 1:21). When a marriage is built upon unbiblical beliefs or nonbiblical philosophies, its very foundation is either ungodly or anti-God. Of course, it is rare indeed for any couple to consciously and willfully adopt such beliefs, but it happens. They carry these beliefs into their marriage and make them the standard of their happiness. But such intimacy with the world alienates a person from God: *"Know ye not that the friendship of the world is enmity with God? whosoever therefore will be a friend of the world is the enemy of God"* (James 4:4).

Since this is true, what can be done? How do the blind and ignorant and those steeped in unbelief ever find the truth? Through God and God alone. *"And you, that were sometime alienated and enemies in your mind by wicked works, yet now hath he reconciled"* (Col. 1:21). God changes the mind! He transforms the intellect.

God also changes the heart. As we saw earlier, *"The king's heart is in the hand of the Lord"* (Prov. 21:1). The heart is the seat of emotion and deeply held convictions. These two things are key players in any marriage. Unless there is a quantum shift toward God-generated feelings and sincerely held convictions about love and commitment, a marriage is hard-pressed to survive, let alone prosper. How is this shift achieved? By working up a feeling? "Falling in love" again? Signing a contract? No, by God's power. And He has the power! He wants to engage it in your life. You have only to ask. It doesn't matter if such glorious change seems out of reach. It doesn't matter even if it seems beyond your wildest imaginations: *"Call unto me, and I will answer thee, and shew thee great and mighty things, which thou knowest not"* (Jer. 33:3).

God changes even the will: *"It is God which worketh in you both to will and to do of his good pleasure"* (Phil. 2:13). This doesn't mean that God overrides the will but that He prepares it for change. He brings you to the point of surrender. He does everything that is needed to lead you to the decision and then says, "Now it's up to you to yield." He works in you "to will." He equips you "to do" of His good pleasure.

You say, "But you don't know my mate. This is the most stubborn, self-willed person I know! He is closed-minded, hard-hearted, and self-centered to the extreme. Can God change him?" Can God change a religious terrorist and serial killer? He changed Saul into Paul. Can God change a man possessed with hundreds of demons? He changed the maniac of Gadara. Can God change you? Yes! Your mate? Without a doubt! Your marriage? Absolutely! *"With men this is impossible; but with God all things are possible"* (Matt. 19:26).

WHY DO YOU WANT YOUR MARRIAGE TO CHANGE?

Consider this important question—why do you want to see a change? In order that *"God be thanked"* or to feel better? Is your motive to bring glory to God or relief to yourself?

While I was pastoring, a wife approached me to visit her back-slidden husband. She expressed deep concern for his spiritual condition. Whereas he once was faithful to church, he no longer attended. Since he lived near the church, I made it a point to drop in on him from time to time and we gradually built a friendship. When I invited him to come to church as my personal guest, he was happy to. I didn't realize how deeply God had been working in his heart through these visits until that morning when I gave an invitation following the sermon. He rushed to the altar with tears of repentance streaming down his face. He confessed his sins and came back to the Lord in a big way. Too big a way apparently. When he began serving as an usher, singing in the choir, driving a church bus, and going soulwinning, his wife came to see me again. "This is *not* what I wanted!" she said. "I wanted a good husband, not a religious fanatic." It wasn't God's glorification she sought, but her gratification. She wanted a kinder, gentler model of her husband, not a radically made-over dynamo for God.

What do you want for your mate? What do you desire for your marriage? If you desire change more for you than for God, it may be that you are wishing for the wrong thing. This can drastically affect your very prayers: *"Ye ask, and receive not, because ye ask amiss, that ye may consume it upon your lusts"* (James 4:3).

I make a practice of asking counselees why they desire counseling. The most common response is "to be happy." I have to tell them, "I can't help you be happy. God didn't call me to make people happy. He called me to make people holy. If I help you be happy without being holy, I haven't helped you at all. But if I help you be holy, you will be happy." Other goals of counseling are relief instead of peace, the instant rather than the gradual, the mate's change instead of my own, and even the expectation that the counselor should guarantee a successful outcome rather than the counselee's focus on personal responsibility in the change process. These are all indicators that the person has not fully surrendered to God's requirements on his own life.

One of the most difficult struggles in the Christian life is conformity to God's will over our own. We naturally desire what satisfies us. It is a spiritual struggle to let go of our desire and seek only God's glory. Even Christ faced this struggle. The most cursory glance at His traumatic experience in the Garden of Gethsemane reveals this. He prayed, *"not my will, but thine, be done"* (Luke 22:42). He was in such agony that the Scriptures record He was sorrowful even unto death, and He sweat great drops of blood. So desperate was His plight that an angel was dispatched to the scene to strengthen Him. What was the cause of such a torturous struggle? The Lord Jesus Christ was facing the agony of the cross, even the loss of His Father's cherished fellowship, and so overwhelming was such a prospect that He prayed, *"O my Father, if it be possible, let this cup pass from me"* (Matt. 26:39). There is a hint, just a hint, that Christ desired His Father to conform to His wishes. But in His heart He knew, and clearly expressed, that it was more important that He conform to His Father's wishes: *"nevertheless, not as I will, but as thou wilt."*

If you find yourself facing this dilemma, if you are in a Gethsemane experience of your own, you ultimately will have to make this choice: change for the sake of self, or change for the sake of God. Bring His wishes into conformity with your wishes or conform your wishes to His.

Paul had God's glory in mind when he wrote, *"God be thanked."* He has set this before all Christians who are in any consideration of seeking a change in their lives or circumstances, including their marriage.

When Paul wrote, *"God be thanked,"* he knew what he was talking about. It is God and God alone who changes our hearts and our homes. But God alone is worth more than all the world can offer, or the flesh can provide. He is there for you and longs to prove Himself strong on your behalf. When you turn to Him, He welcomes you with a loving "I've been waiting for you."

As there is a clear source of truth in this passage, there are also distinct means of truth. One is "doctrine," which is, simply stated, teaching, and in this case, the teachings of Scripture. They are able to make one *"wise unto salvation"* (II Tim. 3:15), *"that the man of God may be perfect"* (II Tim. 3:17), and even cause us to be *"partakers of the divine nature"* (II Pet. 1:4).

Paul was not content merely to introduce a "form of doctrine"; he makes it clear that it was *"delivered you."* This means that someone had to do the delivering. That someone was Paul himself, the servant of God. Life-changing truth didn't merely materialize out of thin air; it was imparted to the Romans through wise counsel and sound teaching. They had wisely positioned themselves under the man of God to benefit from God's truth being funneled through him.

Wise indeed is the troubled couple who determines to seek out a wise spiritual teacher or leader who can help them. *"Confess your faults one to another, and pray one for another, that ye may be healed. The effectual fervent prayer of a righteous man availeth much"* (James 5:16). Contrary to the notion of open confession, I know of no biblical injunction to freely confess your problems to those unaware of your struggles or to anyone who will hear. This passage, however, clearly teaches that a righteous man with an effective prayer life can do much good. Your own pastor is taught in the Word, has a heart of love to help you, and will devote his prayer to your needs. He may want to consult with others and team up with a counselor to find the greatest possible help for you, but he is the logical place to begin. He will seek to deliver the Word unto you.

From an ever-changing sea of conflicting opinions, multiple philosophies, and carnal solutions, the Word of God rises up as an immovable island of solid rock. It never changes with the times or bows before the altar of political correctness. It never defers to the latest chic and trendy pop psychologies that seem to fade as quickly as they appear. It never yields to the attempts of man to dilute or destroy it. For centuries, wave after wave of varied attacks and attempts to corrupt it have beaten against its shores, but the Word stands firm. It is there for you. You don't have to be *"tossed to and fro"* on the sea of life by every wind of doctrine. As countless generations before you, you can find the answers on this island. You can find sanctuary from any storm in the harbor of this island. The godly pastor or wise biblical counselor knows this island better than anyone else does. He lives here. He is the best guide you can find to help you in exploring it and discovering its hidden riches and varied treasure. He knows how to expose them to your eyes and apply them to your marriage.

Like the apostle Paul, he does this by presenting the truth to you and then explaining it. Effective preaching and counseling involve the presentation and explanation of truth.

The presentation of truth is the *"form of doctrine"*; the explanation of truth is that which is *"delivered you."* The difference is significant. The truth can be presented in various ways without the full impact of its explanation. For example, you could arrive at your church this week and hear a recorded reading of the Bible without a sermon or a lesson. Would you have the presentation of truth? Of course. Would it have the power of thorough preaching and sound teaching on the same passage? Certainly not. In the same way, you could find all the help you need for your marriage by reading the Bible for yourself. There is no doubt that the answers are there for the taking. But the struggling pilgrim often overlooks some lofty spiritual truths. Even if they are found, they are not always understood. Even if they are understood, it is not simple to apply them to the specific need. In our counseling ministry to Christian workers, we frequently enjoy a time with learned men who hold graduate Bible degrees in theology and philosophy. Their strength is in their knowledge, but they are often lacking in the application of that knowledge. The explanation of truth is what is needed.

You probably have knowledge of biblical truth. You may even have an active and fruitful ministry of teaching it to others. That doesn't mean that you are successful in applying it to your life or your marriage. This is precisely the reason that we all need the safety of counselors. They see a need you may not see, have a solution you may have overlooked. They provide a strength you don't possess in your isolation and a needed clarity in your confusion. They are provided by God to help bear your burden.

A counselor versed in the Scriptures presents the truth and then, with careful consideration of your needs, explains how the truth can set you free. The source of victory for your marriage then is the Word of God, presented and explained by a servant of God. But even this is not enough without your cooperation in the process.

What about you, the child of God? What role do you play? It is clear from Scripture that you play a very significant role indeed. In Romans 6:16, Paul prefaces his commendation of the Romans with this: *"Know ye not, that to whom ye yield yourselves servants to obey, his servants ye are to whom ye obey; whether of sin unto death, or of obedience unto righteousness?"* Paul makes it clear; the choice is yours. You can choose sin and experience death or you can choose righteousness and experience life. It's not merely a matter of getting the best counsel. Now, you, the counselee, must choose what you will do, and you can do much. You can respond at each level of change: the mind, the heart, and the will. You can *"let this mind be in you, which was also in Christ Jesus"* (Phil. 2:5). You can *"let not your heart be troubled"* (John 14:1), and you can be among the whosoevers who *"will"* follow Christ.

A THREE-STEP PROCESS

Notice the order of Romans 6:17. First "doctrine" was taught, then it went to the "heart," and the result was obedience (*"ye have obeyed"*). To review, "doctrine" refers to biblical teaching to the mind, or intellect; "heart" refers to the feelings and/or convictions; and "obeyed" is the

26

volition or will of man. Therefore, the path of change is first, intellectual, second, emotional and convictional, and third, volitional. The chart below illustrates this three-step process:

The Biblical Path to Marital Victory—*Romans 6:17*

"Doctrine"	Intellectual	Head	Learn It
↓	↓	↓	↓
"Heart"	Emotional/ Convictional	Heart	Love It
↓	↓	↓	↓
"Obeyed"	Volitional	Hand	Live It

To omit a step in this order of things or to begin out of order is to invite delusion and possible disaster. And yet these are the very mistakes made by some. Many wary Baptists, fearing the association with the emotional "excesses" of the Charismatic movement, studiously avoid any feelings in their worship. As a result, they often push their adherents from the "doctrine" step to the "obeyed" step without allowing for the emotions to engage or the convictions to grow, which results in copycat convictions, shallow beliefs, incomplete change, and a performance-type Christianity that produces conformity but little joy.

Many Charismatics, on the other hand, often skip the "doctrine" step, pointing the seeker to the "heart," or emotional step, and then on the basis of feelings demand that he serve God. Because he has missed the step of doctrine, he finds any clarification of his feelings by biblical truth superfluous and even confusing.

Both groups complain of "shooting star," flash-in-the-pan converts, whose decisions on Sunday rarely survive until Monday. Neither has followed the complete plan of Romans 6:17; therefore, the change is incomplete, and the obedience is short-lived.

Most couples I counsel have skipped the doctrine step altogether. Because their relationship began with a euphoric, high-voltage romance, they have little motivation to seek instruction on marriage and may even find the notion laughable. As one young man said to his pastor when challenged about the need of premarital counseling, "What do we need that for? We're in love!" It should be no surprise that most couples spend more time planning their wedding than their marriage. They skip the doctrine step due to the *"ignorance that is in them, because of the blindness of their heart"* (Eph. 4:18).

The solution is to begin where God begins—with doctrine. Strangely, in all my years of counseling, I have never encountered a counselee, married or otherwise, who wanted to begin there. Most people want to begin at the heart stage. They say, "Help me to feel better." Others want to focus on the will. They say, "Help me to act different." But I don't recall anyone coming to me and saying, "Help me to think rightly."

Is it wrong to want to feel better or act differently? Of course not. But will it produce lasting change? Rarely, if ever. Emotional decisions, while intense and moving, are usually temporary if not based on doctrine. Rational, logical decisions to will yourself to change your actions are also short-lived unless fueled by a heart that is moved by truth.

Any marriage that desires a revived relationship must go back to the foundational truths of the doctrine of biblical marriage: *"Ye have need that one teach you again which be the first principles"* (Heb. 5:12).

Doctrinal teaching addresses the mind with sound biblical truth about life issues. Once you know the truth about love and marriage, you have an energizing force that moves the heart and frees the will. *"And ye shall know the truth, and the truth shall make you free"* (John 8:32). Couples that call a time-out to rethink and reshape their core beliefs are light years ahead of those that don't.

At this level, because the change comes from correct doctrine, incorrect doctrine must be identified and *"put off"* (Eph. 4). Misconceptions, lies, distortions, and man-made theories about love and marriage must be clearly identified and abandoned before a couple embraces the truth. This process of putting off presupposes knowledge of the form and shape of the lies that control the thoughts. Painful though it may be, you will have to allow the Word of God to expose these lies, *"even to the dividing asunder of soul and spirit, and of the joints and marrow, and [to be a] discerner of the thoughts and intents of the heart"* (Heb. 4:12).

Teaching should never appeal directly to the heart to change the will. If the emotions are based on a nonexistent or faulty doctrine, they will weaken in time, and the resolve will follow suit. One of the most popular appeals made to married partners is that of recapturing lost feelings. "Come and learn how to fall in love all over again" reads the brochure for one conference. This is not necessarily wrong, just weak.

Another danger of appealing to the heart is that the focus is on renewing the feelings of lost romance. After several trips to the altar of emotional commitment have failed, the seeker may learn to despise any altar. Great discouragement results when one equates the emotional altar with the doctrinal one.

Nor should teaching be addressed directly to the will to change conduct. Once the pressure on the will ceases, the conduct will revert back to its comfort zone. Pressuring a mate to stay with you with threats or coercion will not effect a lasting devotion. Making a decision merely on the basis of duty and obligation won't either. Duty is good, but it is a weak substitute for a doctrinally based, convictionally charged commitment.

The second step in the plan concerns the heart. If the "doctrine" stage is the "learn it" phase, the heart is the "love it" phase. It is the time when fact becomes faith, knowledge becomes conviction, duty is transformed into devotion, and truth becomes personal. It is written about the Hebrews that their *"heart made them willing"* to give (Exod. 35:29) and moved men to work (Exod. 36:2). The apostle Paul describes it as *"doing the will of God from the heart"* (Eph. 6:6).

29

It takes time for the truth of God (especially new truth) to gravitate from the head to the heart. The heart is slow to assimilate these great precepts of God's Word and slower still to convert them into rock-ribbed convictions. For example, the average seeker requires seven exposures to the truth of salvation to trust Christ. Why? Because he has just heard new information that flies in the face of everything he has believed (or hasn't believed) all his life. His initial response typically begins with the first step of denial. "That *can't* be true," followed by doubt, "I wonder if it could be true after all"? If the heart is bypassed at this point and he makes a hasty decision, a life of duty will result. If the heart is moved, his duty becomes a delight and his walk eventually becomes one of devotion.

Truth about Christian marriage, whether learned through personal Bible study, solid Bible preaching and teaching, biblical counseling, or sound marriage seminars and conferences, must be the centerpiece of all approaches to marital change. It is not feelings that set you free or will power that sets you free; it is truth that sets you free. It is not cold, rational choices that set you free; it is truth.

When doctrine enters the mind and finds its way to the heart, change is a natural result. But God's blossoms bloom in His time. To force their petals to open prematurely is to bruise them and damage the plant. Change will require patience to allow the truth of God to do its work, but it is an investment with great returns.

A Threefold Change

As there is a three-step process, so there must also be a threefold change. Unless there is a change at all three levels, it is not complete and will not last.

A friend of mine preached for years as an unsaved man. He had grown up in a preacher's home, attended church all his life, enrolled in Christian schools, Bible college, and seminary, and even served as a pastor for several years, but he was not saved. While preaching on the subject of hell, he came under conviction of his lost condition.

He said, "Jim, I could hardly wait until the sermon was over so I could go forward at the invitation!" And that's exactly what he did. He was the first to respond to his own invitation and met Christ for real. What had happened? His knowledge of Christ was only in the head, but now it touched his heart and changed his life. He experienced a threefold change.

Laura, on the other hand, was different. A teenage girl from a local high school, she attended a Sunday morning service at our church. When the invitation was given, she rushed to the front to receive salvation. Her sobbing and crying was intense. Following a careful presentation of the gospel, I asked, "Laura, do you understand how to be saved?" "Yes," she said. "Do you want to be saved?" I asked. "Oh, yes, I want to be saved!" she exclaimed through her tears. "Are you ready to yield to Christ as your Savior and be saved right now?" Still crying and sobbing, she looked at me and whispered, "No." "Why not?" I asked. "If I become a Christian, I will lose my boyfriend." Laura had understood the truth of salvation. She had even been moved in her emotions to trust Christ. But her will was steadfast. To my knowledge, she has yet to trust Christ as her Savior. Why? Because *"whosoever will"* can be saved. Laura's will was not yielded. She was convinced, but against her will. It is a truism that "A man convinced against his will is of the same opinion still."

When a marriage partner who knows the truth and may even have been moved by it remains steadfastly opposed to any reconciliation, it may be because he has been convinced against his will. This may be traceable to a couple of causes: first, he may not have yielded at his point of resistance, and, second, the timing may not be right for a change.

Most people in sin have a particular point of resistance or an area in life to which they cling and resist any efforts to change. The rich young ruler's point of resistance was obvious. When he approached Christ, asking how he might have eternal life while insisting he had met His initial requirements, Christ said, *"Yet lackest thou one thing: sell all that thou hast, and distribute unto the poor, and thou shalt have treasure in heaven: and come, follow me"* (Luke 18:22). In one discerning stroke, our Lord put His finger squarely on the issue at hand: *"he went away sorrowful: for he had great possessions"* (Matt. 19:22). It has never been part of the plan of salvation that every enquirer must sell all he has and give it to the poor. I often wished as a pastor that it were, but for this man at this time in his life, it was the central barrier to yieldedness.

I once counseled a man who refused to surrender his affair with another woman. He was a mature Christian man and knew the scriptural teaching on this sin and yet had hardened his heart and refused to bend. I counseled two pastors in their sixties who had impeccable records for decades, yet walked away from their wives, their children, their grandchildren, and even their ministry and their call, all for an illicit relationship with another woman. They had a point of resistance.

Now, I am not suggesting that everyone who resists is guilty of sexual immorality; that is merely one of many possibilities. For example, I know of a man who would never give up his tobacco habit. It eventually destroyed his walk with God and even his marriage.

The prodigal son, on the other hand, yielded at his point of resistance. When he came to himself in the pigpen, he yielded to the need of being reconciled to his father. His surrender could well have been related to the timing of God. Certainly he had more time and opportunity to experience the bitter dregs of his rebellion than the rich man in all his wealth and comfort did.

As I said before, there is a difference between the direction of God's will and His timing. Until there is a marriage of the two, the will of God is never ripe and complete.

When we began our counseling ministry some years ago, we welcomed anyone needing help, no questions asked. We soon learned, however, that although a couple may see the need and want it to be fixed as soon as possible, they may not be ready for the fixin'. If there is an agenda, an ulterior motive in coming for counseling, they are invariably disappointed. When they are disappointed, they blame the counselor, the mate, or even God that the problem hasn't been fixed. The problem is compounded because the Moorehead Manor is a crisis counseling center, the last stop for many, and when *that* doesn't work, couples feel there is no where else to turn. They may even justify a marital separation because they feel that they have gone the extra mile in coming for such counseling. Personal agendas and ulterior motives for seeking counseling are indicators that the timing for help is not complete.

God places a high priority on His perfect timing. While Christ shared the desire of Mary and Martha and the disciples to resurrect Lazarus from the grave, He tarried two days. The timing was not right. While God saw the need of saving mankind by sending His Son to die, He waited until *"the fulness of the time was come"* before He *"sent forth his Son"* (Gal. 4:4). His timing was perfect.

God in His infinite wisdom knows the best timing, and while it is difficult for the hurting marriage partner who clearly sees the need of this marriage to wait for His timing, God requires that he do so. He wants that mate to trust Him, and trust is measured more in bad times than good. Don't be *"weary in well doing: for in* due season *[ye] shall reap, if [ye] faint not"* (Gal. 6:9).

There must be a threefold change for lasting victory in your marriage. There must be the acceptance of doctrine that moves the heart to direct the will. Only then will your marriage enjoy the persistent revival you desire.

A man in Florida whose property bordered a causeway heard a loud crashing sound coming from a nearby bridge. Making his way to the scene, he saw that a speedboat had crashed into the pilings of a low bridge, throwing the driver onto the road surface above. He saw a man lying face down in a growing pool of blood. As a crowd gathered, he leaned against the bridge railing and casually lit a cigarette. "Someone ought to do something for that guy," he remarked, as he blew smoke into the air. "He seems to be losing a lot of blood." Shortly, the paramedics arrived and turned the man over. Suddenly, the lackadaisical man dropped his cigarette and screamed, "Oh, my soul! That's my brother! Somebody do something!"

What had happened that so drastically changed the behavior of this man? The truth had gone from his head to his heart and changed his life. And so it is with you. Until the truth of God is understood clearly and is assimilated into the heart, it will never change the will and the life. Until the truth about love, marriage, commitment, and responsibility is understood clearly and is assimilated into the heart, it will never change the marriage.

Oh, may it be said of you and your home, "God be thanked, that ye were the servants of sin, but ye have obeyed from the heart that form of doctrine which was delivered you." It can be.

---

[1] H. Norman Wright, Premarital Counseling (Moody. 1982), 41.

[2] Richard Exley, Perils of Power: Immorality in the Ministry (Tulsa, Okla.:Honor Books, 1988), 85.

[3] Jay Adams, How to Help People Change (Grand Rapids: Zondervan Publishing House,1986), 196.

[4] D. Martyn Lloyd-Jones.

3

Why Are You Married?

Two soldiers went off to war, one to fight for his country, the other to get away from his wife. The latter even wrote his wife a letter, "Would you please stop writing me so I can enjoy this war in peace?" Do you think both of these men deserve the same recognition and honor?

While motives do not excuse wrongdoing, they are important to any of life's endeavors. In many ways, why we do what we do is as important as the act itself. Why did you enter the marriage relationship? Why do you *remain* there?

Motives reveal much about the future of any marital venture. One of the most common causes of marital discouragement is expectations that are never met. Your motives for marriage will have a direct bearing on your expectations. If your motive for getting married is selfish, then your expectations will follow suit, and *"hope deferred maketh the heart sick."*

A poor motive will also produce a weak commitment to the marriage. After all, if your selfish motives aren't realized, and they are the only things holding you to your mate, why stay in the marriage? Like the nervous bank robber who hastily scrawled a note to the teller, "Don't stick around! This is a mess-up!" any marriage partner whose primary motivation is selfish will also refuse to "stick around" in the face of a marital "mess-up."

Motives also determine true priorities. If your primary motive is happiness, you will see your marriage as a source of fulfillment and your mate as the primary agent to produce it. You will find yourself constantly bound by your unseen motivations and you will gravitate to that end.

Most importantly, motives determine God's blessings upon your relationship. A vital consideration at the Judgment Seat of Christ will be your reasons for serving Him. Each believer will be required to give account of his motives for serving Christ. As Robert Ketcham has said, "Our secrets, our motives, and our decisions all come out under the fire of His holy eyes. We will tell Him *all;* not only *what* we did but *why* we did it!"[1] I was shocked when, as a young pastor, I realized that I was training my people to serve God for the wrong reasons. While reading Matthew 6 one day, it came to me that the wrong motives may bring a reward, but the wrong reward. If a man fasts, gives, or prays *"to be seen of men,"* or *"that they may have glory of men,"* Christ is clear that in each case, *"they have their reward."* And what is it? *"To be seen of men."* In other words, if a Christian's motive in serving God is praise, recognition, or the applause of men, he receives it, but that is the substance and end of his reward. The motives of the heart are to be seen of men or to be seen of the Father. Likewise, the rewards are distinguished one from another; one either receives the praise of men or the pleasure of the Father: *"Take heed that ye do not your alms before men, to be seen of them: otherwise ye have no reward of your Father which is in heaven"* (Matt. 6:1).

Every person who has ever married had a particular motive in mind at the time of his wedding. It can vary from one individual to another, but it is very important to the marriage, to its expectations, its commitment, its priorities, and God's very blessings. What motives did *you* bring to the altar? Why did *you* get married? Why do *you* remain married? Here are some of the most common reasons for getting married and staying married. Consider whether they may be your own.

WHY ARE YOU MARRIED?

ESCAPE MOTIVATION

First is the escape motivation, often seen in the life of a person who has had a bad childhood and desires to get away and start over. I once counseled a wife who told me, "I grew up in an abusive home and my eighteen-year-old boyfriend was a knight in shining armor. He rode into my life on a white charger. He swept me off my feet and carried me off into the sunset, promising me a new beginning." Twenty years and five children later she was sad to discover that the problems of childhood she thought she had escaped actually had made their abode in her own heart. She had not avoided them after all.

Another wife once confided, "I got married to get away from home. My parents fought constantly, and I hated the depressive atmosphere. When I was sixteen, my boyfriend promised to take me away from all this. I married him, but I realize now it was more to get away from home than to be with him." Eighteen years after marrying, this wife realized that the very things she had hated most in her parents' marriage she was duplicating in her own. She eventually made the decision to leave her husband and her children to be with another man who would "take me away from all this."

It is not unusual for people to repeat the same problems in their marriage that they hated in their parents' marriage. They may not understand the reasons. They cannot understand why abused children become child abusers, why victims of molestation become molesters, why children of alcoholics become alcoholics. One reason is that a person becomes what he thinks about the most. As a man *"thinketh in his heart, so is he"* (Prov. 23:7). When he thinks on the sinfulness of a man, he becomes like that man, even duplicating the sin he hates most. By focusing his thoughts on the sins of his parents and stewing in his anger and hatred, he is becoming like the very thing he hates most. Leaving home in a hasty "emergency exit" marriage will not take one away from the problems; he merely takes the problems away with him. When a person thinks on Christ, he enjoys the peace of God: *"Thou wilt keep him in perfect peace, whose mind is stayed on thee"* (Isa. 26:3). This constant reflection on Christ becomes the means of molding a Christian into His image. Through this process one is *"conformed to the image of His Son"* (Rom. 8:29).

Rehabilitation Motivation

During a marriage conference I once conducted, I distributed a written survey for the participants to fill out. One of the questions on the survey was "Why did you marry your mate?" One man responded, "I knew she could help me," while another answered, "I needed her." These men apparently married out of a need to be rehabilitated. They had the misguided notion that if they got married, the unseen monsters of sin and failure from their pasts would be magically conquered by a good wife.

I have heard similar remarks from would-be wives who, when faced with obvious deficiencies of their suitors, minimize their shortcomings with idealistic simplicity. Despite chronic alcoholism, a hair-trigger temper, a proven inability to hold a job, a prison record, or a general lack of fitness in a prospective mate, these girls chalk it off to a past gone awry, and assert, "I know he has some problems, but I can help him. The power of love will change him into the man of my dreams."

Whether the goal is to be rehabilitated or to do the rehabilitating, these people fail to realize that only God can ultimately change another person. *"For it is God which worketh in you both to will and to do of his good pleasure"* (Phil. 2:13) and *"we all . . . are changed into the same image from glory to glory, even as by the Spirit of the Lord"* (II Cor. 3:18). Husbands who look to their wives for help in changing are looking to the wrong source. And wives who see themselves as having the power to change their husbands end up feeling responsible for them.

Nursery Rhyme Motivation

What little girl who plays with her favorite doll doesn't dream of the day she will hold a real baby in her arms? It is a natural and God-given desire for any couple to enjoy the delights of parenthood, but when the children become primary, a spouse often becomes secondary. This was obvious to me when one wife confided, "We came for counseling to hold the marriage together for the kids' sake." Forty percent of married couples report that having children at home is the factor preventing a divorce.

I can picture the "child-centered" couple in their declining years. There they sit on the front porch in their trusty rockers. Even in their eighties, they still call each other "Mom" and "Dad." They have little to look forward to except a visit or call from the children and grandchildren. They have neglected each other for the children's sake so long that they have lost touch with each other.

GRATIFICATION MOTIVATION

The gratification motivation is probably most common among young men whose overactive glands have short-circuited their brains. When one respondent of my survey revealed why he married, "I wanted a woman!" I couldn't help but chuckle. I pictured a brutish, grunting caveman with a club over one shoulder, dragging his prize by the hair into his lair, all the while drooling saliva from his chin.

This need of sexual gratification is not an unusual motivation to marry. The nursery rhyme motivation is more common among girls, and this one is more often seen among the guys. They are feeling the power of overactive glands and are "on the verge with the urge to merge." They see marriage as a legitimate outlet for these drives.

It is not wrong to see marriage as an acceptable means of conquering the flesh. In fact, the apostle Paul advised youth to marry if necessary to accomplish this very thing: *"To avoid fornication, let every man have his own wife, and let every woman have her own husband"* (I Cor. 7:2); but this must not be the primary reason for marriage. Why? Because the basic focus is self-centered. It is selfish rather than selfless. God intended that marriage be a safe haven where this basic human need can find satisfaction, but no marriage will prosper unless this desire is subjected to God's higher goals.

OBLIGATION MOTIVATION

This brings us to the obligation motivation, or the feeling of being pressured into getting married. Much of this pressure originates with a fashionable social mindset that "getting married" is the thing to do.

A common experience of seniors in college is "senior panic," the fear that their senior year is the last chance to find a mate and time is running out. Sometimes there is even some apparent spiritual pressure applied by well-meaning family members. "We are praying for you that you find a mate and give us some grandkids" or "When are you going to get married?" or "What do you think about so and so? Wouldn't he/she make a good mate?"

And there are even sexual obligations that create a sense of urgency as well. As one wife responded when I asked her why she had tied the knot, "We were promiscuous before marriage and I felt obligated to marry him." She married despite the fact that she really didn't want to.

SECURITY MOTIVATION

One woman who totally depended upon her husband for her livelihood was devastated when he died. Her whole world fell apart and she went into a long-term depression. She simply couldn't cope with the notion that her provider was no longer around to care for her. Her failure was not in depending on her husband but in depending on her husband's provision over God's. A sense of depression over such a loss is normal and grieving is healthy, but this emotional collapse in the face of the loss of a mate is a clear indication that the focus is wrong.

If you enter into marriage with the hopes of finding the security of acceptance, companionship, or financial support in a person instead of in the Lord, you are doomed to disappointment.

It is not wrong for a wife to have confidence in her husband. But it is wrong for her to place her faith in him above her own faith in God. If a wife develops a strong faith in God, she will trust Him to work through her husband to meet her needs. But the husband is only one of a vast variety of means that God can use to that end.

Husbands are sometimes threatened by this line of reasoning. They like the fact that their wife leans on them and resent any teaching that diminishes that dependence. A wise husband, however, will lead his wife to a stronger and stronger faith in God for the inevitable day of death's separation. Just as a loving husband plans for his widow's financial well-being through savings and a will, he should plan for her spiritual well-being by leaving her a legacy of spiritual faith.

How about you? Why did *you* get married? Why do you *stay* married? If your motives determine the very quality of your marriage and the blessings of God, then it would behoove you to rethink your motives.

There are various higher motives for marriage revealed in the Scriptures, but for our purpose, let's consider three.

Glorification Motivation

For committed Christians the ultimate consideration for any undertaking is "Will it glorify God?" Bringing praise and honor to Him is uppermost in their minds. Their desire, more than anything else, is to follow Paul's admonition, *"Whether therefore ye eat, or drink, or whatsoever ye do, do all to the glory of God"* (I Cor. 10:31). While in college I had the privilege of working at a Christian camp under Dr. Ken Hay, one of America's foremost camping ministers. For two summers, every morning, I would stand at the flagpole with all the other staff and campers and recite I Corinthians 10:31 aloud. I must confess that at the time it was little more than a nice thought, but now it has become a life principle. If it is important to eat and drink *"to the glory of God,"* how much more important is it to marry to His glory?

This commitment to glorify God is best made before the wedding but can be made at any time. Is your primary consideration for your marriage to bring glory to God?

MINISTRY MOTIVATION

When the Lord Jesus Christ came to earth, He said, *"The Son of man came not to be ministered unto, but to minister, and to give his life a ransom for many"* (Matt. 20:28). If your marriage is to be "Christian," it must be Christlike. If it is to be Christlike, it must be permeated with Christ's sacrificial spirit of ministering.

Man's primary ministry on this earth is not witnessing, teaching, or even pastoring. These are all worthy and lofty goals to be sure, but God has given every husband and wife a priority of ministry in meeting the needs of their own mate.

To fail to make this a motive in your marriage is to take the first step toward allowing your relationship to degenerate into a marriage of manipulation instead of one of ministry.

ILLUSTRATION MOTIVATION

Even a brief look at Ephesians 5 will let the reader in on one of God's chief designs for marriage. The clue is in a tiny two-letter word. *"The husband is the head of the wife, even as Christ is the head of the church . . . as the church is subject unto Christ, so let the wives be to their own husbands. . . . Husbands, love your wives, even as Christ also loved the church."* The model of the wife's submission and of the husband's love for his wife is Christ's relationship to the church. For the Christian to understand marriage, he must first understand this special relationship between Christ and His church. This is the high ground of any discussion on marriage.

Just as Christ's love for the church is the model upon which marriage is based, it is also the motive for marriage. The wife is to be motivated to submit in such a way as to illustrate the submission of the church to Christ. The husband is motivated to love his wife in such a way as to illustrate the love of Christ for the church. This sends a powerful message to a lost world.

Christ has always been concerned with reaching the world through the testimony of Christian relationships. He said, *"By this shall all men know that ye are my disciples, if ye have love one to another"* (John 13:35). In His famous priestly prayer, He prayed for unity among the brethren and for its very powerful effect on the world: *"That they all may be one . . . that the world may believe . . . that they may be made perfect in one: and that the world may know that thou hast sent me, and hast loved them"* (John 17:21, 23). Jesus knew that the world watches the Christian and that the message of love and unity between believers sends a powerful message to the lost. It can actually be a means of their salvation.

While living in navy housing, my wife and I lived next door to a young couple with a new baby. They drank, cursed, and partied constantly. Sometimes our pictures hanging on the wall between our apartments would tremble from the loud vibrations of their rock music. After a few months Francine approached my wife, Sandra. "I notice that you never swear and you and your husband seem to have a very special relationship. Why is that?" Sandra was able to witness to her about her faith in Christ. Francine trusted Christ as her Savior and it wasn't long before her husband followed her. Not too long after that, it was my joy to ordain him into the gospel ministry and he became a pastor.

When a husband loves his wife *"as Christ loved the church,"* he visualizes for the world how much Christ loves His church. When a wife submits herself to her husband, she visualizes to the world how the church is subject unto Christ. This provides a powerful attraction to this loving Christ. When the world sees Christ's love bring unity to two totally different personalities, and they see His power to produce and sustain supernatural love in their relationship, it speaks volumes. This is what they want. This is what they have been searching for. What a testimony!

The ultimate sin of Christians' divorcing is not the damage it does to the marriage, the destruction of a home, or the devastation it brings upon children. These are terrible things and cannot be overstated, but at least the Christians who are involved have the message of salvation and knowledge of the power of God to rebuild their lives. But the onlooking world is left without a picture of God's power and His love. For them the fact that Christians are divorcing at an unprecedented rate even higher than that of the world means that the church and God and Christianity don't offer much more hope or power to build love than the world does. A precious candle of hope is then put under the bushel of divorce. A dying world is doomed to stumble on in darkness because one of God's special lights has been extinguished.

The Grand Artist of time and eternity paints a masterpiece demonstrating His love and His power through the Christian marriage. God desires this work of art to be held aloft for the world to behold. It is in this context that God receives the greatest glory from today's marriages. This is the highest motive, the noblest cause, and the most holy of reasons for the existence of a marriage. To seek to illustrate Christ's love, the church's submission to Him, and His unifying power is to raise marriage to a level unknown to the man-centered masses. A Christian marriage is a powerful visual aid. What a ministry! What a blessing to others and what a challenge to mediocre marriages floundering in worldliness.

Indeed, God has a high purpose for His painting of marriage, but how sad it is to see it sullied and marred by the awful specter of divorce. The real damage is not to the canvas or to the various paints used or even to the brushes, but to the Artist Himself. The tragedy of divorce is not that lives are wasted, dreams are dashed, or feelings are hurt. These are terrible without a doubt, but there is a greater sin; His painting is destroyed. His purpose is unrealized. It's as if someone has taken a knife to a Rembrandt or a work of Michelangelo . . . but worse . . . far worse! God's goal of illustrating His love through Christian marriage has been reduced to a mere statistic. Instead of driving by the church wishing that their marriages could be like those within its walls, the world knows that there is very little difference in the power in the church and the power they possess. There is little to convince the world of their need for a God who makes so little difference. Your marriage may not be perfect, but it can be powerful; and its greatest power and influence come from its fulfillment of God's purpose for its existence.

Perhaps you are reading this and fearing an end to your marriage. What can be done? One thing that can be done is to rethink the very purpose for your union with your mate. Why did you get married? Why *are* you married? Why do you remain married? Are your motives noble enough? Is your aspiration lofty enough? Are your sights set high enough? If not, there is good news!

Even if your marriage began for all the wrong reasons, with the worst of motives or intentions, God is more interested in the present and the future than the past. *"Better is the end of a thing than the beginning thereof"* (Eccles. 7:8). Let's face it; few Christian young people have thought through all these motives and weighed their heart's impulses in light of them. How many engaged youth take time to analyze their inclinations? When I stood at the altar watching my beautiful bride glide down the aisle to take my hand, I did not have thoughts such as "Ahhh, here comes an opportunity to display God's love to the world!" I'm sorry. That just did not happen. My thoughts were akin to "Hot dog! Something *good* is about to happen to you!"

Perhaps Paul alludes to these emotions when he writes, *"When I was a child, I spake as a child, I understood as a child, I thought as a child"* (I Cor. 13:11). At some point, however, we must all come to the place of realizing the need to replace childish notions with mature ones: *"When I became a man, I put away childish things"* (I Cor. 13:11).

Have you put away the wrong motives for your marriage? If not, you can now. Truly, *"better is the end of a thing than the beginning."* And better is the end of your marriage than its beginning. It's not too late to make a difference. Much depends on your answer to the question "Why are *you* married?"

_____

[1] Robert T. Ketcham, quoted in Carl G. Johnson, *The Account Which We Must Give* (Schaumburg. Ill.: Regular Baptist Press, 1989), 15.

4

The Meaning of Marriage

The Son of man came not to be ministered unto,
but to minister.
Matthew 20:28

The full significance of any undertaking is best understood in the original intent of its founders. A brief look at the history of some key United States institutions is a case in point. Both Harvard and Princeton were begun primarily to train preachers of the gospel. By studying the original intention of their founders, one can easily see how far afield they have strayed over the years. To understand the importance of the U.S. Constitution, it is necessary to go back to what the Founding Fathers designed it to accomplish. To judge current laws in the light of the intentions of the framers of the Constitution is to understand their desires by keeping their writings in the context of history. Those original intentions form the basis of U.S. laws.

Ministry

The same is true in marriage. Nobody can fully understand or appreciate the significance of this wonderful institution unless he goes back to the original intent of its founder. We know that God is the founder; the question is, what did He envision for marriage? What did He see as its purpose? Fortunately, we are not left to guess about this. God has left clear instructions in His Word. According to the Scripture, the meaning of marriage in a word is ministry: *"Submitting yourselves one to another in the fear of God"* (Eph. 5:21).

What is this submission of which Paul writes? It is not referring to lines of authority in the marriage or the structure of leadership in the home. We know that because in the next few verses he makes a clear case that the man is the head and the woman is to follow. The lines of authority are clearly established.

The message of this verse is that the husband should submit to the needs of the wife and the wife should submit to the needs of the husband. Paul expands on this thought in Philippians 2. Any couple who wants to enjoy a good marriage will be encouraged by his inspired words: *"If there be therefore any . . . comfort of love . . . in lowliness of mind let each esteem other better than themselves. Look not every man on his own things, but every man also on the things of others"* (Phil. 2:1, 3–4).

The intriguing thing about God's approach to marriage in these passages is that He studiously avoids mentioning the needs of the reader. Unlike the literature of our age, the Bible ignores this altogether. Eighty percent of all books on marriage sold in Christian bookstores are bought by women. The vast majority of these books appeal to the readers' rights or needs. Titles include *How to Be Happy Though Married, What Wives Wish Their Husbands Knew About Women* (a lot of wives buy that book*), What Husbands Wish Their Wives Knew About Men* (many men buy that one). Of course, this approach sells books, but it does not develop a burden for ministering to the needs of your mate. Rather, it encourages the manipulation of your mate to meet your own needs.

God's approach is entirely different. He does not encourage the reader to dwell on his needs but rather to dwell on his responsibility to meet his mate's needs; and a good way to discern those needs is to study the responsibility of each to the other. For example, a reading of *"Wives, submit yourselves unto your own husbands"* reveals that a basic need of the husband is the need to be followed. God made the husband to lead and he is most fulfilled when he does.

When God says, *"Husbands, love your wives,"* He is revealing that a basic need of the wife is to be loved. God made the wife to be loved and cherished by her husband, and she is most fulfilled when she is. He does not say, "You poor husband. You need someone who believes in you." He does not say, "You poor wives. What you really need is some strong man who will love you." He doesn't address the *needs* of the reader at all. To do this would encourage self-pity and self-centeredness. Rather, He addresses, in no uncertain terms, the *responsibility* of the reader.

It is a truism that "the teaching of rights breeds rebellion. The teaching of responsibility brings revival!" God emphasizes what we are to give, not what we want to get. This is ministry.

Think about it! When you focus on your needs in marriage or push for your rights, you place yourself in an awkward position. First, you are dependent upon the response of your mate for your satisfaction. His response is the only guarantee of your joy. On the other hand, if your fulfillment is determined by what you do instead of what is done for you, you gain some measure of control over your level of enjoyment in marriage. You can always choose to minister; that choice is yours and nobody else's. When you do it, how you do it, and how much you do it is under your control.

Secondly, if you are dependent upon your mate for satisfaction and he fails to come through, you may find that the resulting desperation can prompt you to use pressure and scheming to get him to meet your needs. This recourse to manipulation is a painful way to satisfaction, yet a way of life for many marriage partners.

It is a commitment to marital ministry that God calls for, not to manipulation. This ministry of meeting the needs of your mate will keep a marriage revived and a heart encouraged.

NOT MANIPULATION

I mentioned earlier that I worked for a couple of summers at a Christian camp in South Carolina. Many troubled young people from the inner city found their way into the camping program. These children were neglected, abused, and generally as unloved as any people I have ever known. As a result, they presented a real challenge to me, a teenage counselor. This challenge was never more clear to me than during one memorable week of camp. One of my responsibilities was to oversee a table of these hardened youth at each meal. On one occasion, we had a meal that required ketchup. One industrial-sized squeeze bottle was provided for each table. I looked at Frankie, an eight-year-old boy at the other end of the table, and said, "Would you pass the ketchup, please?" He looked back at me with strangely defiant eyes and said, "I ain't had none yet!" I said, "Okay, go ahead and have some, and when you're finished, pass the bottle down here." I thought this would be an opportune time to introduce this little urchin to good table manners, so I continued, "The proper response, however, would be, 'May I have some first, please?'" Rather than show gratitude for this lesson in etiquette, he seemed to resent it. He locked his eyes onto mine, and without blinking, turned the bottle upside down and began squeezing. The ketchup started to mound on his plate, but he kept squeezing. I saw a power struggle forming between this insolent eight-year-old and me, a mature eighteen-year-old, and I felt the first stirrings of "righteous indignation." It started in my feet and began moving upward through my body. In the meantime, the ketchup had reached a stage of critical mass and was now dripping over the edges of his plate. My indignation was now up to my knees. He continued pumping until the telltale sucking sound showed that the bottle was empty. At this point my righteous indignation was at waist level. No little kid was going to tell an eighteen-year-old veteran camp counselor what to do. Without blinking, I told him, "You're going to eat every bit of that!" I just knew he would be awed and cowed at such authority. "Oh yeah," he responded. "Who's gonna make me!" The indignation was now at chest level. I stood to my feet. He put his hand under the plate, and with his unblinking eyes still glued to mine, slammed it into the table with a "ka-wham-yow" sound. Ketchup flew everywhere. My indignation had now gone over the top.

I started around the table to reach him, but he saw me coming and darted out the screen door. I was hot on his tail. Several times he was just inches beyond my reach when he would dart in another direction. His short little legs gave him the advantage in the underbrush of the woods, and fortunately I lost him. I say "fortunately" because if I had caught him I probably would be in prison instead of writing this chapter.

After a while I came upon him sitting on a log by the lake. I started to sneak up on him for the surprise lunge when I noticed something peculiar. His bony shoulders were bouncing up and down. As I got closer, I understood why. He was sobbing his little heart out. At that point, the Holy Spirit got my attention and sobered me quickly. I quietly sat at the other end of the log without speaking. He sensed that I was not a threat and stayed where he was. I slid down the log, put my arm around his shoulder, and said, "You've got a lot of pain in that heart of yours, don't you?" That really turned on the tears, but it also opened his heart to mine. He began telling me things that shocked me.

I learned that his mother was a prostitute and his father was her pimp. They were both drug users and dealers, and regularly they used his bedroom to ply their trade. They never told him to go to bed, to get up, or to get ready for school. Food was never prepared. He was never told to take a bath, never had his clothes washed, and was never spanked. They rarely spoke to him except to tell him what to do, never kissed him, never hugged him, never touched him except in anger. In short, he was never loved. His parents didn't even know he was at camp and didn't care. The only way he knew to get attention was to "act out." In his defiance at the table, he was reaching out in the only way he knew.

And what of me? Mr. Maturity? All I could think about was that a child was making me look foolish, and nobody was going to get away with that! God showed me the coldness of my heart and the selfishness of my actions. I realized that my entire motivation was to feel good about myself by getting even with this "punk kid." I had set out not to minister to him but to be ministered to. I could not even think about ministering to him because I was too busy manipulating him for my own selfish reasons. Until I saw this awful truth, I was hardened to Frankie's needs.

Until you see this truth, you will be hardened to your mate's needs.

HOW TO MINISTER TO THE BASIC NEEDS OF YOUR MARRIAGE PARTNER

THE MINISTRY OF THE WIFE: SUBMITTING

If the basic purpose of a husband is to lead, a basic need is to be followed. The wife is strategically placed to meet that need by submitting to her husband's leadership. Teachings about submission in marriage create much contention and animosity. This may be because of a heavy-handed approach to the subject that many women view as self-serving chauvinism. Let's face it, men, there has been a lot of abuse of this doctrine. One extreme form of this teaching insists that a woman is to obey her husband "no matter what he tells her to do." The logic here is that he is responsible to God while she is responsible to him. If he orders her wrongly or even sinfully, and she obeys, he bears sole responsibility for her action. Strangely, some well-known Christians teach this.

It is a fascinating fact of Scripture that the same man who wrote, *"Submit yourselves to every ordinance of man for the Lord's sake"* (I Pet. 2:13), when he was faced with civil magistrates who ordered him to no longer teach or preach in the name of Christ, thundered, *"We ought to obey God rather than men"* (Acts 5:29) and promptly disobeyed the law. Why? Because he recognized that all human authority is derived from a higher authority. The highest authority is God as revealed in His Word.

If man creates a law that is contrary to God's Word, what should we do? What if the U.S. government to appease other religions passed a law that Christians could no longer witness of their faith in public? (I predict that law is coming.) What should be our response? We have not only the right to disobey but also the obligation to disobey just as Peter did. But we should also be prepared to go to jail as Peter did. There is a lesson here for both the wife and the husband. The wife should submit to her husband in every case except when there is a clear violation of God's authority. (The burden of proof is upon the wife to be assured of this.) The husband should not flaunt his authority or abuse his power by heavy-handed demands that violate either the letter or the spirit of God's Word.

Many form opinions on the subject of submission on the basis of experience. A young person may grow up in a home in which extremes of submission were on display: the groveling doormat of a wife with an overbearing, brutish husband, or the Battling Bertha who cracks the whip over a Harvey Milquetoast. From the home of the groveling wife, a young lady may assert, "No man is ever going to treat me like that!" From the home of Harvey Milquetoast, a young man may emerge, saying, "A woman needs to be put in her place." Experience may not be the best teacher after all.

Others may form their opinions from popular teaching, philosophies, faddish cultural trends, or even feminist beliefs. But whatever the source of anti-submission beliefs, the results are clear. They produce rebellious children, encourage homosexuality, destroy God's plan of family harmony, discourage male initiative, encourage laziness in husbands, and even drive some husbands away from their wives. *"It is better to dwell in a corner of the housetop, than with a brawling woman in a wide house"* (Prov. 21: 9).

Why should you submit to your husband? First, because it is a command of God. This is not optional. It is not a suggestion. It is a command. If for no other reason, every wife should want to obey her God. Obedience brings His blessing; disobedience brings His displeasure. In fact, to know that you should do this and refuse is to sin: *"To him that knoweth to do good, and doeth it not, to him it is sin"* (James 4:17).

A second reason for submission is that it expresses trust in God. That is the meaning of Paul's admonition in Ephesians 5:22: *"Wives, submit yourselves unto your own husbands, as unto the Lord."*

The issue then is the object of your submission; it is not the husband but Christ Himself. Your submission is an expression of trust in Him: *"For after this manner in the old time, the holy women also, who trusted in God, adorned themselves, being in subjection unto their own husbands"* (I Pet. 3:5). The expression of the trust of these holy women was their submission to their husbands. When you submit to your husband, you are demonstrating your trust in God. When you submit through His appointed authority, you show your trust in the Appointer.

The issue has never been the character of the husband but his position as the duly appointed authority of God over you. It is not the perfection of his character in question, but the purity of his position.

In fact, God seems to go to the extreme to demonstrate that what is crucial in submission is not so much trusting *in* a man but trusting *through* a man. When Christ submitted to Pilate, it was not because of Pilate's sterling character or his depth of spirituality. It was not because of him at all; it was *in spite of* him! Christ's trust was not in Pilate but through him to God.

When Pilate became frustrated with Christ's refusal to answer him, he arrogantly asserted, *"Speakest thou not unto me? Knowest thou not that I have power to crucify thee, and have power to release thee?"* (John 19:10). Our Lord was not impressed. He knew where the power originated. *"Jesus answered, Thou couldest have no power at all against me, except it were given thee from above"* (John 19:11). It is clear then from Scripture that Christ's submission to Pilate's authority was not an expression of trust in him, but trust *through* him to God. Christ *"committed himself to him that judgeth righteously"* (I Pet. 2:23).

It is in this context of submission to unfair spiritual authority (read I Pet. 2:21-3:6) that the Christian wife is exhorted to submit to an unworthy husband. Peter chooses a key word to bridge the gap between Christ's submission and the wife's: *"Likewise, ye wives, be in subjection to your own husbands"* (I Pet. 3:1). This is a direct reference to the example of Christ so powerfully portrayed in the preceding verses.

The point of submission, then, is first and foremost to the object of your trust. God is the ultimate object while submission through a man is merely the expression of that trust.

God is marvelously glorified when a wife trusts Him to work through her appointed head.

This is not to say that submission is easy or painless. Quite the contrary. For Christ it meant the cross. It may for you as well. But the ultimate glory of man is that of the cross (Gal. 6:14), and the ultimate glory to God comes from the choice of a godly wife to submit to her husband as an expression of trust in Him.

Third, when you obey God with a meek and quiet spirit of submission, you exert a far greater positive influence on your husband than you realize. God goes so far as to say that through submission a woman can influence her husband for good. *"Likewise, ye wives, be in subjection to your own husbands; that, if any obey not the word, they also may without the word be won by the conversation [behavior] of the wives"* (I Pet. 3:1). A tongue-in-cheek definition of submission is "the art of ducking so God can hit your husband." You never duck better than when you are on your knees in prayer. This is an expression of your trust in God. This biblical approach will go a lot further than the world's approach of nagging. *"A continual dropping in a very rainy day and a contentious woman are alike"* (Prov. 27:15). In other words, if you nag your husband, you're a drip!

The problem with this meek approach in marriage, according to the thinking of many wives, is that it takes so long. Some well-placed pressure seems to produce much quicker results. So do drugs for that matter, but the long-term effects are costly. God's way is usually not for the quick change but for the long haul.

Fourth, when you submit to your husband, you minister to his needs. God made him to lead. Your willingness to follow encourages him to lead. It will require much patience on your part, dear wife, but if you will trust God to work through your husband, even his failures, God will honor your faith.

THE MINISTRY OF THE HUSBAND: SACRIFICING

Paul captures the essence of the husband's ministry to the wife in one phrase: *"gave himself."* This is sacrifice. A husband must offer his wife the sacrifice of leading her. He is to be the *"head of the wife."* You say, "How is leading a sacrifice?" There is a high price to pay for leadership, any leadership. It makes no difference whether you lead a country or you lead a home; it will cost you. At the very least it will cost you the price of being criticized. Someone put it well: "If you're getting kicked in the rear, it means you're in the lead!" Or to put it another way, "If you're leading, you will get kicked in the rear!"

While in navy boot camp, I led a company of eighty-two men. I was responsible for getting them up, putting them to bed, and even drilling them in marching maneuvers. This tedious job of sounding cadence while practicing drills apparently seemed very appealing to my second platoon leader. Since he followed me in the chain of command, it seemed fitting to him that he should enjoy the reins of leadership as well as me. Finally his big chance came; I was called away to another part of the base and left the company in his care. An hour later when I returned, I had no difficulty finding my company. They were marching in a dozen different directions, colliding with one another, all the while giggling like a pack of school children. A couple of them were even lying on the ground, engulfed in paroxysms of uncontrolled laughter. Off to one side stood the poor platoon leader, a picture of total failure. When he saw me, he ran to me and said, "Binney, am I ever glad to see you! This is not as easy as it looks, and you can have the job." He discovered what every leader must learn; there are times when the romance of leadership is eclipsed by its burdens. Carrying that burden and enduring the pain is part of the sacrifice of leading.

Your wife needs to see that you have a genuine desire to seek the Lord. When a wife sees her husband on his knees, or with his Bible open, it gives her a warm, settled assurance that God is in control, which gives great security.

Second, she needs to know that you have some settled, established, not-for-sale-or-trade convictions—convictions that are based on the Word of God. *"A double minded man is unstable in all his ways"* (James 1:8). A wishy-washy, hot today, cold tomorrow belief system creates enormous instability and fearfulness in the heart of your wife. Your living one way in church to please the people there and folding under the pressure of the world for the same reason will not create confidence in your wife. For example, a conviction that church involvement is nonnegotiable is paramount. Leading your wife and family to church each week will provide enormous stability and confidence. Many men are failing in this regard.

Above all, there must be love in your leadership. We will talk more of this in following chapters, but this cannot be overstated. For many years, the child-rearing experts assailed parents with the need of using the right techniques, following the proper order of things, and conforming to prescribed steps of child discipline. As a result, millions of parents concentrated on how to "cross their t's" and "dot their i's," but they forgot to spend time with Junior. They worked at providing a good living but neglected to teach him by example. Now the "experts" have apologized for this unbalanced approach. Recent studies have revealed that more important than all these things in parenting is that the child grows into adulthood with a pervasive, deep-seated sense that Mom and Dad love him. The greatest need of your wife for which you are personally responsible is to give her that same assurance.

Another sacrifice required of the husband is that of loving his wife *"as Christ also loved the church, and gave himself for it."* At first reflection, it seems that something is wrong with equating love with sacrifice, and that is part of the problem. Many men, even Christian men, have bought into the notion that love, while being priceless, is also costless. It offers much and requires little. The Bible describes love not in terms of feelings but of action, and the action involves a sacrifice. The greater the sacrifice, the greater the love.

This raises an interesting question. Who loves the most? The teenager in the mall glued to his girlfriend, whose every expression of love flows from effusive feelings, or the husband of fifty years who cares for his bed-ridden wife, who cannot even recognize him, let alone return his affection? There is something to be said for such sacrifice and faithfulness, but few, it seems, are saying it.

Some men are fond of reminding their wives what they have given up for them. "I gave up Monday Night Football to take you to your mother's! And what thanks do I get?" Such motives reveal not a sacrifice but an investment. If you give to receive, it is to achieve a desired end. If you give willingly, even eagerly, with no hope of getting something back, that's a sacrifice. What have you sacrificed lately for your wife?

CONCLUSION

What is the meaning of marriage? It is ministry. Sadly, it is the missing ingredient in many troubled marriages of today. If there is one common thread encountered in counseling married couples, it is that they lack any sense of ministering to their mates. Rather, they have made a lifetime commitment to getting their mate to minister to them. If Christ came *"not to be ministered unto,"* should we approach marriage with a goal of getting our needs met? If Christ *"came to minister,"* should we approach marriage for any lesser reason?

5

Ministering to the Greatest Need of Your Husband

In the last chapter, we saw the importance of having a ministry to your mate. In this chapter and the next, we will show you the greatest need of your mate. This will give you a clear goal in your ministry to him or her. You will learn how to understand your mate, help him or her, and as a result, bond to him or her with a spiritual glue.

One source of understanding is the Bible itself. We look again at the greatest piece of literature ever penned on the subject of marriage, Ephesians 5. This is the Magna Carta of all thinking on the subject. It originated with God, was passed on to the apostle Paul through the marvelous process of "inspiration," and then was recorded in print for generations to come, including yours!

The world has tried to understand marriage from a totally different perspective. As a result, their understanding is lacking at best and warped at worst. The world has an insufferable amount of ignorance about the opposite sex because they do not have the same source of knowledge that we have. They look within themselves; we look up to God. What does He say?

The Husband's Greatest Need: To Be Followed

"Submitting yourselves one to another in the fear of God" (v. 21). We learned that this refers to submitting to the needs of your mate. The need

of each marriage partner is revealed in the responsibility of the reader. As you read Ephesians 5, you will notice that the greatest need of the husband is to be followed, respected as a man, and believed in as a leader.

"Wives, submit yourselves unto your own husbands" (v. 22) refers to your responsibility of following his spiritual leadership. You are to *"submit,"* he is your *"head,"* and you are to be *"subject"* unto him (vv. 22–23). And all this is to be done as "unto the Lord." Remember that this submission is a spiritual function and requires the spiritual assistance of the Holy Spirit. But knowing this does not erase the fear and hesitancy of many wives. They have a natural aversion to this concept. There are several reasons for this.

WIVES FEEL RESPONSIBLE FOR THEIR HUSBAND

Susan's face registered shock and blank numbness. As the full significance of my question sank in, I observed the progression of self-realization. A telltale grin began to spread over her features, and even before her tongue could form a response, her countenance had revealed her answer. The question? "Do you feel responsible to your husband or *for* your husband?"

My question had been prompted by her admission to various tendencies to control her mate, born out of a sense of shared significance with him. His success was seen as hers, and his failure was a source of embarrassment and shame. She took full responsibility for his recent affair and had a pattern of taking personal affront to any criticism directed at him. She expressed anger at him through nagging, criticism, and attempts at revenge.

She was frustrated with his foot-dragging passivity in decision making and chronically took the lead—at first with his permission, then from a sense of obligation at his default, and finally in open defiance of his wishes.

My question had uncovered her propensity to control and a misplaced sense of responsibility for her husband.

Consider this question for yourself. How would you respond? Do you feel responsible to your husband or for him? I have posed this same question to countless wives in counseling sessions and marriage seminars over the years; and in numerous cases, a uniform pattern has emerged. Like Susan, many others harbor similar feelings.

WIVES FOCUS ON THEIR HUSBAND'S HUMAN PERSONALITY INSTEAD OF HIS DIVINE POSITION

God has created three divine institutions: the state, the church, and the home. Over each of these institutions He places a human leader. He makes it clear that in each case the leader has a divinely appointed position and He robes his title with immense dignity. Government leaders are said to be *"ministers of good"* and *"ordained of God"* (Rom. 13); pastors are called *"elders"* to denote their maturity, *"bishops"* to show their function, and *"shepherds"* to show their responsibilities. The church is told that they *"have the rule over you"* (Heb. 13:7) and are to be obeyed. The husband and father is called the "head" of the wife and her submission to him is compared to the submission of the church to Christ.

God's plan for each of His institutions is harmony. He desires for everyone under His appointed leader to live in unity. Unity, not merely union. You can tie a dog's tail to a cat's tail, then throw them over a clothesline and have union, but it sure isn't unity! You can tie a man and a woman together with legal papers and matrimonial knots, but that doesn't guarantee unity either.

God's plan of unity is realized through His appointed leaders. Two things are required to accomplish this: first, the integrity of the leader's reputation and, second, the purity of the follower's evaluation. The leader is responsible for the integrity of his reputation; the follower is responsible for the purity of his evaluation of the leader. Enter Satan. He will attempt to disrupt this unity by defeating the leader, tempting him to sin in some way. At the same time he will attempt to defame the leader to the follower; he is the *"accuser of the brethren,"* who begins to sow discord by planting base, dishonoring thoughts in the minds of the follower, especially the wife. She lives with this man, knows what he does with his dirty socks, sees him kick the dog and yell at the kids, so the Devil whispers in her ear, "You don't have to submit to that! Look at him. He's just a sinner!" The Devil has just tricked her into shifting her focus from his divine position to his human personality.

Mankind has a natural aversion to authority. Nobody likes to be told what to do by anyone else. This innate, fleshly dislike of authority is exploited to the full by the media. They tap into it regularly. Watch how often those in authority are represented as less than good. The media do this purposefully. Television has never been about intellect but emotions. Fear, anger, lust, and greed are staple fare and the underlying theme behind the majority of programs. Anger can easily be aroused by emphasizing the injustices perpetrated on people by those in authority. Recently I learned of a "man on the street" interview that asked the respondents to say the first word that came to mind when they heard these words: congressman, policeman, dad, and evangelist. You will notice that each of these titles represents one of God's three divine institutions. The leading response for congressman was "corrupt," for policeman, "brutal," for dad, "deadbeat," and for evangelist, "immoral." Where did Americans get such a low opinion of authority? The answer in large part is the media. By a constant, unrelenting attack on authority to get ratings, they have blurred the line in the viewers' minds marking the difference between authority's position and their personalities. Nothing is said about God's opinions of these positions. When this imbalance of emphasis continues, resentment of all authority is the natural result. When is the last time you saw a policeman portrayed as a hero, a politician shown as a true public servant, an evangelist applauded, or a husband esteemed? I have made a point of studying TV commercials that feature a man and woman duet, especially a husband and wife combination. Without exception, when this occurs, the husband looks foolish. Perhaps the purpose is to sell products to women, but the result over time is that constant ridiculing of the man's human personality diminishes his divine position.

This portrayal has damaged the husband/wife relationship severely. It has diminished the wife's respect for the spiritual office of her husband. Because she has been conditioned to focus on her husband's human personality instead of his divine position, she does not hesitate to encroach upon his office to achieve her goals. The *"holy of holies"* becomes just another compartment in the tabernacle, the ark of the covenant becomes an object of curiosity rather than of worship, and the vehicle carrying the ark is just another wagon requiring the hand of Uzzah to keep it from toppling. A casual view of holy things has always led to unholy familiarity and from unholy familiarity to tragedy. Studying a husband's divine position will go far in reestablishing that respect and give the wife a biblical basis for a spiritual submission to him.

LACK OF FAITH IN GOD

Many wives lack faith in God to work in the heart of their mate, and through him to them. As the idealization of husbandhood gives way to the reality of human nature, some wives become disillusioned—not only in their husband's failure to meet their expectations but also in God's apparent absence. This twofold disappointment can degenerate into a life-view of isolated, self-sufficient independence. An unspoken code evolves: "If I don't make a difference, no one will."

A major reason for this void of faith is the wife's view of God. Some wives have come to see Him as remote and distant, others see Him as uncaring, and yet others view Him as capriciously cruel because He allows the neglect or mistreatment they suffer at the hands of their husband. In any case, they interpret their pain as a justification to take matters into their own hands.

What is needed? A return to, or perhaps the beginning of, a strong realization of the loving sovereignty of a holy God. After all, contrary to the view of some, He *is* in control. He worked through the circumstances that brought you and your husband together. *"The lot is cast into the lap; but the whole disposing thereof is of the Lord"* (Prov. 16:33). He controls in the placement of godly leaders and husbands, even the placement of an oppressive husband into your life. Consider this amazing fact: *"The most High ruleth in the kingdom of men, and giveth it to whomsoever he will, and setteth up over it the basest of men"* (Dan. 4:17). And why does God set up base men in positions of authority? Although we can never fully understand the ways and thoughts of God, it is clear that His purposes are for our good (Rom. 8:28). The apostle Paul realized it when he wrote, *"But I would ye should understand, brethren, that the things which happened unto me have fallen out rather unto the furtherance of the gospel"* (Phil. 1:12).

Some wives lose sight of this and forget that God can use the foolishness and sinfulness of a husband's personality to form the Lord's divine character in him, themselves, and thus accomplish a holy purpose. Instead, in a desperate scramble to avoid pain, they gradually yield to the temptation of manipulating their husband to get their own needs met.

Unfulfilled Expectations

Another reason for a wife's misplaced drive to control her husband is related to unfulfilled expectations. Because she expected certain things and he has failed to deliver them, she becomes discouraged. If *"hope deferred maketh the heart sick"* (Prov. 13:12), then the discouragement from the postponement or cancellation of an unrealistic expectation produces a sense of loss. That in turn can drive the frustrated wife to attempt to press for the fulfillment of those expectations in her husband. For example, from childhood we have been taught that life's events bring happiness. Remember "And they lived happily ever after"? Add to that the theme of love songs, romance novels, and "boy meets girl" movies, and many women are set up to expect what men cannot realistically and perpetually deliver: heart-pounding, pulsating, throbbing romance. Granted, the first two to three years of marriage will deliver this gossamer promise of youth, but as one disenchanted wife lamented, "I married an ideal, I got an ordeal, and now I want a new deal." If the wife places an unrealistic expectation of romantic love upon her husband and he fails to deliver it voluntarily, she may be tempted to wring it out of him. Bringing her sizeable portfolio of womanly wiles into play, she may try flattery, cajoling, threatening, isolation, tears, and even the locked bedroom door. Both the wife's spirit and the marriage itself would benefit from a careful rethinking of her expectations of her husband.

How a Wife Can Biblically Follow Her Husband

Respect Him as a Man

It is sometimes easier for a woman to follow someone she doesn't know very well. The pastor and the policeman evoke respect, but it is easy to get comfortable with a long-time husband and to approach the whole duty of following him with a cavalier attitude. That is why the emphasis of the Scriptures is to follow your own husband: *"Wives, submit yourselves unto your own husbands"* (Eph. 5:22). This makes it very personal and brings it home to where you live.

A man has a natural need to establish his manliness, and there is no end to the foolish ways he follows to accomplish this. Many men seek to measure their manhood by the amount of beer they consume. Others point to the amount of weight they can lift or the size of their biceps. Even sexual conquests, professional achievements, and the amount of money accumulated are priorities for many misguided and insecure males. But God has a better way. He wants to provide their need for significance, but in a spiritual way, and it is not found in the world but in their own heart and home.

Any man's sense of value is met first and foremost by his relationship with God. When he experiences the fullness of God and all the blessings of His precious fellowship, he can feel great contentment. But that is God's direct ministry to man. God also has an indirect ministry . . . through the wife.

As the wife submits to her husband, God uses her to underscore his value. "My wife believes in me" is a knowledge that generations of men have understood. A famous football player made a spectacular play that won the game in the closing seconds. The stands were packed with thousands of adoring, screaming fans while millions watched by TV. He ran down the sidelines clutching the game-winning ball, stopped at the 50 yard line, and gazed into the stands, oblivious to the adulations of the crowd. The TV screen was suddenly filled with the face of one smiling woman. The announcer informed the viewing audience that this was the player's wife. The hero of the hour grinned and saluted his wife with a thumbs up signal. She smiled back at him and returned his salute. He then ran off holding the ball aloft in victory. He demonstrated to the world the value that a husband places upon his wife's approval. Every husband understands that built-in need.

As a wife, you can do much to help meet that need of approval. Let him know that you need him and depend upon him. A chivalrous sense of protecting the fair maiden from harm is not limited to the knights of the Round Table. It is alive and well in the heart of every decent man. Your self-sufficiency will destroy dependence. After all, if you're too competent and you've got it all together, why do you need him? The writer of Proverbs wrote, *"Feed me with food convenient for me: lest I be full, and deny thee, and say, Who is the Lord?"* (Prov. 30:8-9). It is a basic truth of Scripture that self-sufficiency destroys trust. Sometimes a full belly is the worst thing for our relationship with God, and a full purse is the worst thing for a wife's relationship with her husband.

You should give serious thought to the value of working outside the home. There is a growing disregard among women for full-time careers, especially among Christian women. When asked, "If you had enough money to live as comfortably as you'd like, would you prefer to work full time, part time, do volunteer-type work, or work at home caring for the family," 85 percent of women at large did not desire to work outside the home. "Most women today prepare for careers, but they still put family first. . . . And more than a few actually want full-time homemaking."[2] (Even 74 percent of feminists agreed with these women.) From these results, I would conclude that wives want to be *"keepers at home, good, obedient to their own husbands, that the word of God be not blasphemed"* (Titus 2:5) and to *"marry, bear children, guide the house, give none occasion to the adversary to speak reproachfully"* (I Tim. 5:14). This survey shows a growing awareness among women that home is the place to be.

When you as a wife look to your husband for your provision, you call up the best in him. He responds to your need of being provided for and protected. He knows you believe in him and he doesn't want to let you down. This response of a man is well documented in Scripture. First Peter 3:1–6 will bear out the truth that a man responds positively to a trusting wife.

That is not to say that some extenuating circumstances may require the wife to work outside the home, but this should be at the direction of the husband rather than merely a desire to "have more." Studies show that the advantages gained by working outside the home are minimal.

One important quality of leadership is providing for the needs of the family. When your husband assumes the responsibility for generating the finances for the family, he is exercising his leadership. When you work outside the home, your boss (the source of your money) may take on greater importance than your husband.

Another way of showing your husband respect is to accept his decisions in your spirit. A little boy was told to sit down by his father. He had to be told a second and even a third time before he obeyed. When he did sit down, he frowned and said, "I'm sitting down on the outside; but I'm standing up on the inside!" To accept your husband's decisions in your spirit means much more than this. It means honor and respect. A wife's spirit greatly influences her husband's ambitions. Such knowledge may have prompted Ralph Waldo Emerson to pen these words: "A man's wife has more power over him than the state has." Just as criticism and a review of past failures do great harm to your relationship, praise will do great good.

One of the greatest ways a wife can follow her husband is to . . .

Reverence Him as a Leader

"Let . . . the wife see that she reverence her husband" (Eph. 5:33). This means to revere and respect his position of authority. This can be done in several ways, all of which build the strength of the marriage.

Reassure your husband that you trust God to work through him and that you believe that you see evidences of that. Let him know that you respect his authority because it comes from God. Many husbands struggle with the idea of being competent leaders. Your faith will strengthen your husband's hands to be a good leader for you.

Express words of trust to your husband: "I know you will take care of us. You always have" or "I know God gave you to me." Words such as these will go far in showing your husband that you reverence his leadership.

Encourage him to hold onto his God-given goals when things look rough. Every marriage has down times when the clouds block the view of the sun. A little light from your smile will go far to dispel the darkness.

Seek spiritual counsel from your husband. Appeal to his leadership by expressing your need of spiritual direction. This will strengthen your relationship, encourage him to study the Bible, honor God, and set a godly example for your children. With your words, you can encourage others to admire your husband. Talk about reverence!

You will have a tremendous influence on your husband as you minister to this primary need of his. Your obedience to God in this matter will free Him to bless you and your marriage. Become an expert on how to meet your husband's needs and you will experience more joy than you will specializing in your own needs.

Submit "as unto the Lord"

The high ground for any discussion on the wife's submission is the lofty motive mentioned by the apostle Paul: wives are to submit *"as unto the Lord"* (Eph. 5:22). This is not a call for equal submission to the husband and to the Lord. As Lloyd-Jones notes about this phrase, "It does not mean, 'Wives, submit yourselves unto your own husband in exactly the same way as you submit yourselves unto the Lord.' It does not mean that, because that is going too far. . . . We are all the bond-slaves of Jesus Christ . . . but a wife is never told to be the slave of her husband."³ Such a low life-view has spoiled the spirit of submission that Christ desires for the Christian wife.

Submission is not to be from a sense of man worship, feelings of inferiority, or even binding duty. God desires that *"whatsoever ye do, do all to the glory of God"* and that includes your submission to your husband. Submission to your husband is an expression of your submission to God. You are to do it for Christ's sake and His glory. This will raise the ministry of submission from the dark valley of duty to the bright mountaintop of delight.

Conclusion

The author of a popular book on marital needs advocates that the wife separate from the husband as a means to improve her marriage: "Anyone considering a separation should simply take that action and then work on the marriage."⁴ Such a blanket endorsement of the philosophy that the end justifies the means may be a reflection of the thinking of the world, but it does not reflect the thinking of God. The Bible encourages the wife to take responsibility for the outcome of the marriage. *"Depart not"* (I Cor. 7) is the counsel of God's Word.

God's plan, on the other hand, is that husbands be *"won by the conversation of the wives; while they behold your chaste conversation coupled with fear"* (I Pet. 3:1–2). This is a far cry from the desperate manipulation of a wife who feels she has the right and the responsibility to change her husband.

Remember Susan, the chagrined wife at the beginning of the chapter? As she applied these principles to her marriage, she discovered that not only was she freed from an undue burden but also her husband's spirit was drawn to hers. He had been waiting for this change in her. Perhaps your husband is waiting also.

---

[1] Frank S. Zepezauer, "Women Want Careers with 'Mommy Track,'" *Insight on the News* 12, no. 47 (1996): 30.

[2] Zepezauer.

[3] D. M. Lloyd-Jones, *Life in the Spirit: In Marriage, Home, and Work* (Grand Rapids: Baker Book House, 1975), 101.

[4] Willard F. Harley Jr., *His Needs, Her Needs,* (Grand Rapids: Fleming H. Revell, 1986), 35.

6

Ministering to the Greatest Need of Your Wife

Just as the greatest need of the husband is revealed in the Scriptures, so is the wife's. As the key to understanding the need of the husband is to study the responsibility of the wife, the key to understanding the need of the wife is to study the responsibility of the husband.

The Wife's Greatest Need: To Be Loved

"Husbands, love your wives. . . . So ought men to love their wives. . . . Let every one of you . . . so love his wife even as himself" (Eph. 5:25, 28, 33). The theme that threads its way through God's instruction to the husband is that the wife needs to be loved. Husbands, it is up to you to meet that need. The kind of love that God is speaking of is *agape* love. You have probably already experienced other forms of love, but this love requires special attention. God has provided a manual of instructions for this purpose. The manual for the software I am now using to write this chapter runs over four hundred pages. And this is supposed to be the age of the quick and easy. By contrast, God's manual consists of only nine verses of Scripture. What do they say?

How to Love Your Wife

To understand how to love your wife, you must understand Christ's love. *"Husbands, love your wives . . . as Christ . . . loved"* (v. 25). To understand Christ's love is a supernatural undertaking rather than a natural one. It requires that you *"know the love of Christ, which passeth knowledge"* (Eph. 3:19). Sound tough? Not really. God has made it supremely easy to know of His love for us: *"Husbands, love your wives, even as Christ also loved the church, and gave himself for it"* (Eph. 5:25).

Husbands are commanded to love like Christ loved the church and *"gave himself for it."* You can turn to many sources to try to understand the high subject of love, but Scripture is the best place to go and the best way to know exactly what kind of love your wife needs. It is a . . .

SACRIFICIAL LOVE

The evidence of biblical love is always measured by its costs. When God wants to show how much He loves us, He always reminds us to consider how much it cost Him. *"For God so loved the world, that he gave his only begotten Son"* (John 3:16) and *"God commendeth his love toward us, in that, while we were yet sinners, Christ died for us"* (Rom. 5:8).

The evidence of your love, like Christ's love, is your sacrifice. Christ sacrificed much on the cross for His bride, the church. He gave up His pride when He hung in shame. He surrendered His friends when they *"forsook him, and fled"* (Matt. 26:56). He gave up all relationships, even and especially the one He enjoyed with His Father. He lost His primary source of joy when His Father had to turn His back on the sin His Son had become. Christ loved the church so much that He let go of all comfort and suffered as no man suffered. Ultimately, He sacrificed His very life. *"Hereby perceive we the love of God, because he laid down his life for us: and we ought to lay down our lives for the brethren"* (I John 3:16). If you want to understand the love of Christ, you have only to look at His sacrifice. If you want your wife to understand your love, there must be a greater measurement than that of desperate attempts to communicate how you feel. If we *"ought to lay down our lives for the brethren,"* what greater love is there than that? Obviously, God wants the "brethren" to include your wife; He featured her above all others as the object of your sacrifice. That's why He said to *"love your wives, even as Christ also loved the church."* What have you sacrificed lately for your wife?

When King David wanted to honor God for His goodness, he went to offer a sacrifice to Him. A well-meaning friend offered to give him everything he needed for this act of devotion. The king wisely objected, saying, *"Nay; but I will surely buy it of thee at a price: neither will I offer burnt offerings unto the Lord my God of that which doth cost me nothing"* (II Sam. 24:24). The king knew that it was no love at all if there was not a cost involved in it. A wise husband will conclude the same thing. The greatest evidence of love is not what you feel or what you get from another; it is what you give. More than that, it is what you sacrifice.

My dad taught me this lesson firsthand. My mother suffered from Alzheimer's disease for years. At first she merely forgot a few things here and there, but then it became difficult for her to speak coherently. As things regressed, she ultimately could not even recognize him. Against his better judgment, but because she required constant care, he put her in a nursing home. He visited her daily but grieved that he could not be near her round the clock. He hired a live-in nurse and moved Mom back home. He once said to me, "Jimmy, my prayer is that I might outlive your mom by one day." I watched him tenderly care for her, helping her in and out of bed and dressing her, even brushing her hair and hand feeding her while wiping her mouth for her. I marveled at the love he had for her because she could never return his love. For years, he continued this selfless ministry, never wavering in his devotion to her. She continued to deteriorate and finally on Christmas Eve, 2002, she breathed her last. Even then, Dad was by her side, holding her hand and comforting her. He loved her to the end without receiving anything in return.

The time will come in your marriage when you are called to make sacrifices for your wife. When that happens, it will show her how much you love her, and your gifts of love will strengthen your marriage just as Christ's gifts have strengthened the bonds between Him and the church.

SATISFYING LOVE

It is not enough to love your wife with a love that satisfies you. It is her satisfaction that is important in godly love. Just as the satisfaction of the church was Christ's objective in His expression of love on the cross, so must your wife's satisfaction be your goal. The husband *"nourisheth and cherisheth"* his wife even as Christ nourishes and cherishes the church (Eph. 5:29). The word "cherish" has the meaning of protection. It is pictured by the mother hen gathering her chicks under her wings, where it is warm and soft, protecting them from any danger. Your wife needs this kind of love. She wants to feel your warmth and protection and she needs it as the "weaker vessel."

You cherish her when you treat her tenderly, when you seek above all else to understand her sensitivity, when you treat her with honor. God holds this to be so important that He gauges answered prayers according to the husband's faithfulness in fulfilling this need: *"Ye husbands, dwell with them [wives] according to knowledge, giving honour unto the wife, as unto the weaker vessel, and as being heirs together of the grace of life; that your prayers be not hindered"* (I Pet. 3:7). God sees great value in your wife.

And what great value she has! *"Who can find a virtuous woman? for her price is far above rubies"* (Prov. 31:10). "Virtuous" means "morally pure, of moral excellence." When you find a girl who lives purely under God (not someone with a perfect past as much as someone with a present purity), you have found something of enormous value. Modern man rephrases this verse to read, "Who can find a beautiful woman . . . a shapely woman . . . a talented woman . . . a brilliant woman . . . a personable woman," but God bypasses all these things to esteem virtue. What do you esteem? Your love for your wife is to be like God's love. To have a love like God's is to esteem what God esteems. *"Man looketh on the outward appearance, but the Lord looketh on the heart"* (I Sam. 16:7). When God looks on the heart, He places great value on it. Not only does He say that virtue is worth more than rubies, He says that your wife's soul is worth more than the whole world! *"For what shall it profit a man, if he shall gain the whole world, and lose his own soul?"* (Mark 8:36). When God measures the worth of your wife's soul, He places it on one side of the scale, and on the other side He places all the gold of this world. He adds the silver, the diamonds, the real estate, the stocks and bonds, and all the other assets that every millionaire, businessman, corporation, and nation on earth possess. Then He declares, "Your wife's soul is worth more than all that!"

I once went into an antique store to buy a desk for my son. In my ignorance, I saw the things for sale as a bunch of junk (antique lovers spell that "junque"). I saw a desk that would work, though it was a bit beat up. "How much is it?" I asked, thinking maybe ten dollars. "Three hundred dollars," the clerk answered. I showed my ignorance of antique shopping in my response. "How can that be?" I said. "It's got dings and scratches all over it. How did you come to put that price on it?" She gave me an aristocratic look that thinly veiled her disdain for such ignorance while she said, "The store owner put that price on it because some people will pay it." Maybe they would, but I wouldn't. When a buyer agrees with the owner about the value, he has no problem paying top dollar. When a husband agrees with his wife's owner about her value, he has no problem sacrificing for her. That is godly love: loving what God loves, the way God loves. It is agreeing with God about her value. It is cherishing her.

Why Love Your Wife?

On the surface this may sound like a foolish question, but it is an important one. There are many selfish reasons to love another. Christ's reasons for loving the church, by contrast, describe the highest motives in love and hold incredible lessons for the husband. Why did He love the church? *"That he might sanctify and cleanse it with the washing of water by the word, that he might present it to himself a glorious church, not having spot, or wrinkle, or any such thing; but that it should be holy and without blemish"* (Eph. 5:27–28). Notice His goal for the church. He wanted to sanctify it. This should be the husband's goal for his wife.

As Christ set out to minister to the spiritual needs of the church, so you are to minister to your wife. You love her when you help her to be sanctified, which means simply to be set apart for a special purpose, to become more and more like Christ. Years ago a deformed prince commissioned an artist to bring a block of marble into the courtyard of his palace to carve a statue of him as he would appear if he were normal. The sculptor began his project, and before long the face of the beloved prince began to emerge. But the body was not that of the deformed prince but of a normal and upright prince. After the sculptor cleared away the debris, the prince was seen approaching the statue. He studied it for a moment and then backed up to it, placing his hands on the hips of the statue. He strained to straighten his back. He continued this until his muscles were cramped. He continued this for days, weeks, even months. One day he walked up to the statue, backed up to it, and to everyone's delight, touched the back of his head to the back of the statue's head, his shoulder blades to the statue's shoulder blades. He had literally conformed himself to the image of the statue. That is what sanctification is—becoming *"conformed to the image of his Son"* (Rom. 8:29). Loving your wife with the motive of sanctifying her is to help her to look at Christ, to study Him, and to compare herself to Him in every way she can so that she can gradually be conformed to His image. This is the highest motive of love, to help your wife become more like Christ. Only when this goal enters the heart of the husband will that marriage realize its full potential.

WHEN TO LOVE YOUR WIFE

It may be better to ask "How long to love your wife?" It is shocking to know that while the Bible teaches that love *"faileth not"* and *"suffereth long,"* modern love seems hardly to outlast the echoes of the words "till death do us part." It is disappointing to see instead of the biblical model of love that *"suffereth long,"* couples trading their mate in for a fresh one much like a man trades one car in for another. The length of married love today certainly differs from that of the Scripture. But the godly *agape* love of a husband for his wife is best understood by comparing it to Christ's love for the church. And what a lasting love that is! Romans 8 lets us know that nothing, absolutely nothing, can quench the love of

Christ. *"Who shall separate us from the love of Christ? shall tribulation, or distress, or persecution, or famine, or nakedness, or peril, or sword? . . . I am persuaded, that neither death, nor life, nor angels, nor principalities, nor powers, nor things present, nor things to come, nor height, nor depth, nor any other creature, shall be able to separate us from the love of God, which is in Christ Jesus our Lord"* (Rom. 8:35–39). This concept is so unlike the "here today, gone tomorrow" love of so many romanticists. How much better is God's love than a love that is so fragile that it cannot withstand the breeze of neglect, let alone the gales of tribulation. If you love your wife with the love of Christ, there is not a power from earth or hell that will be able to stop it. When you consider the wedding altar and hear one of the most famous questions of all time, "Will you love her in sickness and in health, in poverty as in wealth, and forsaking all others, keep thee only unto her so long as you both shall live? Do you so promise?" do you realize the seriousness of your answer? But even beyond what these vows require, will you love her *"as Christ loved the church and gave himself for it"*?

CONCLUSION

Every wife needs to be loved, not with the vaporous, flimsy sentimentalism of ill-considered emotions, but with the love of Christ, by a man who has love borne out of knowledge and a commitment forged in a study of Christ's love. The greatest need your wife will ever have is your love. What a wonderful ministry you can have. What a wonderful marriage you can enjoy!

7

Myth-Information About Love and Marriage

A battle-weary couple with a twenty-year marriage had just completed a week of counseling with me at the Moorehead Manor. The wife said, "We have learned so much this week that we never knew before. We are the typical couple I guess who married in haste. We received no premarital counseling and were never taught about marriage. If only we had known then what we know now, our marriage would have been so much better."

This couple had made a hasty decision based on incomplete information. Like most couples who come to me for counseling, they were lacking some basic knowledge when they married. Unfortunately, it is impossible to go back in the past and start over with new knowledge. But while you can't change the past, you can change the present and the future by learning now what you need for these times.

Part of this learning for the future though requires that you adjust your focus, that you find a different source of truth that can serve you better than the fuzzy thinking that motivated the young girl above. This is not always easy.

In an age when more people get their notions of love and marriage from television than from church it is no wonder that much confusion whirls around the topic. When the Love Boat replaces the Love Book as the authority on relationships, it is understandable that darkness will prevail over light and myths triumph over truth.

It has always been the conflict of the ages, this battle between truth and error. It has been played out with a disturbing consistency on the field of matrimony. On the one side is arrayed the world, the flesh, and the Devil. It would seem a conspiracy exists between them to package error so slickly that it has a universal appeal. Their deception offers instant gratification and avoids, even denies, any consequences from indulgence.

On the other hand is truth. As plain and unattractive as the cross is, it promotes sacrifice rather than gratification, offers penalty for sin instead of pleasure, and promises happiness more for the afterlife than for the present. It is often presented so frankly that its very nature is offensive to many. This is why Paul asked the question *"Am I therefore become your enemy, because I tell you the truth?"* (Gal. 4:16). Truth is rejected by many like King Ahab because it often *"doth not prophesy good concerning me, but evil"* (I Kings 22:8).

Because of this lackluster appeal even Bible-believing Christians are often lured into the enticements of error. They find themselves drawn into the world's thinking without realizing it. Their need for fulfillment and their drive for gratification often blind them to the value of prickly truth.

The battle for the soul is a crucial one. Much hangs in the balance of the outcome. How can this battle be won? The Bible's strategy is simple but effective: identify the lie, reject it, and replace it with the truth. This was God's advice to Jeremiah: *"See, I have this day set thee over the nations and over the kingdoms, to root out, and to pull down, and to destroy, and to throw down, to build and to plant"* (Jer. 1:10).

As God commissioned Jeremiah and prepared him for service, He told him that he would have to undo some common thinking before he could redo with right thinking. In fact, He used four negatives to two positives. Talk about negative preaching! He told Jeremiah that he would have to root out, pull down, destroy, and throw down before he could begin a program to rebuild and replant.

God underscored this by utilizing two powerful metaphors: a garden and a house. The ultimate goal with a garden is "to plant" and the ultimate goal with a house is "to build," but before either can be done, some preparatory work is required. For the garden to be planted, the soil needs preparation by getting rid of the weeds; Jeremiah was told to "root out" these weeds before planting new seeds. For a new house to be built the old house needs to be removed and the rotting timbers replaced. Thus, Jeremiah was commanded to "pull down," to "destroy," and to "throw down" the old to make way for the new. To plant among weeds or to build over decaying lumber is foolish and counterproductive.

Some marriages are like a beautiful garden. They abound with lovely blossoms whose fragrance can be enjoyed by all who walk the manicured paths between them. Other marriages are like a sturdy, well-built house, whose stability and beauty attract many to drop in for a visit. Everyone wants such a marriage, but many fail to realize that it takes a lot of effort to plant a garden and to build a house. The apostle Paul alludes to this when he writes, *"For we are laborers together with God: ye are God's husbandry, ye are God's building"* (I Cor. 3:9). Laborers? That sounds like work. You mean it takes work to build a marriage? Whatever happened to effortlessly "falling in love"? Isn't love something that just happens to you? Something over which you have no control?

Apparently not. Rather than falling in love, the Scriptures advocate growing in love: *"And the Lord make you to increase and abound in love one toward another"* (I Thess. 3:12).

This is a notion opposed to the gospel of the media mavens and romance novelists. And it is this very disparity that compels any student of love and marriage to pull up short and check his sources. Where do your beliefs about love and marriage originate?

If the source is wrong, the teaching is wrong: *"Beware lest any man spoil you through philosophy and vain deceit, after the tradition of men, after the rudiments of the world, and not after Christ"* (Col. 2:8). The truth is, many Christian marriages are spoiled by wrong teachings. Their gardens are grown over with weeds and their house is falling down around their heads.

What is to be done? The obvious place to start is to identify the lies and myths about love and marriage, which have been around for centuries. This can be challenging because they come from so many sources. As Ken Abraham writes,

> Couples who remain married must realize sooner or later (and the sooner the better) that many of their premarital impressions of marriage were little more than marital mush, the stuff of which myths and fairy tales are made. Some of these myths are handed down from our parents. We pick up others from friends, relatives, books, magazines, or movies.[1]

Identifying the source is not enough however; Abraham also warns of the need of acting on the myths themselves: "Regardless of their source, the sooner you dispel marital myths, the better chance you have of marital bliss."[2]

Dispelling these myths is a labor of love that should know no bounds and spare no energies or effort. Studying to be a *"workman that needeth not to be ashamed"* is hard work indeed.

To that end, I am going to have to shoot some sacred cows in this writing. There may be a lot of blood so have your mop handy. We are about to identify some of the most popular myths that I encounter in my marriage counseling and that are causing many marriages to fail.

MYTH 1

THE HONEYMOON FEVER WILL LAST FOREVER

Is it true that love will never wane or die? Of a thousand young people surveyed at a Christian college, 56 percent believed so, even that "love is permanent, lasting a lifetime." Despite the fact that past relationships have failed, that love has faded, and that love has been erased from the memory, many youth believe that the marriage bond will be different, that love will never waver. The Lord Jesus Christ qualifies this: *"Because iniquity shall abound, the love of many shall wax cold"* (Matt. 24:12). It appears then that love can definitely decrease, but why?

It is the natural order of things to go through cycles or seasons. *"To every thing there is a season, and a time to every purpose under the heaven"* (Eccles. 3:1). This can be seen clearly in the Christian life. For the new convert it begins at the season of new faith after first experiencing salvation. Then he encounters sin and its accompanying guilt. If untreated, these can result in backsliding. But his new temple occupant, the Holy Spirit, loves him so much that He convicts him of his sin until he repents and experiences revival in his heart. Salvation, sin, backsliding, and revival are normal seasons for the Christian life.

Parenting also has seasons. When the new baby arrives, all is well amidst much cooing and gurgling. Then the baby turns two. Uh-oh! Thankfully, the child outgrows the twos but then . . . becomes a teenager! Teenagers eventually grow up and become mature adults. Infancy, terrible twos, teen years, and adulthood are normal seasons for the human life.

A pastor upon first accepting a call to a church experiences what is euphemistically termed the "honeymoon period." After two or three years, though, the glow of a new congregation and pastoral duties fall victim to the inevitable routine of the daily grind. The routine is often replaced by drudgery, which through the intervention of God is followed by a new vision and renewed purpose. The honeymoon period, the routine, the lean years, and the renewal are normal seasons for the pastoral life.

Marriages likewise often follow a well-worn path of predictability: first comes romance, followed quickly by reality. Then comes regression, and with God's help, rekindling. These seasons are normal for the married life.

Let's look at these seasons of marriage more closely: the graph below charts the four seasons of marriage for easy reference.

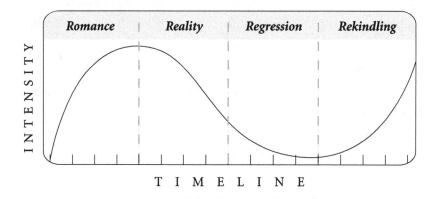

ROMANCE

The romance season is full of promise and excitement. It begins with the first attraction, continues into courtship and the first two to three years of marriage. This is not surprising since it takes at least two full years to become thoroughly acquainted with another person's true character.

The chief characteristic is pleasurable emotional intensity. But this emotionalism is a pied piper, who can easily lead one astray.

The power of this season can be seen in the lyrics of popular songs of the past. "Before the dance was through, I knew I was in love with you!" sang one authority on the subject. Another singer crooned, "I didn't know just what to do, so I whispered, 'I love yew'!" But one group from the sixties takes the trophy for the most impetuous approach: "Hello, I love you, won't you tell me your name!"

This season is rife with clammy palms, dry tongues, wobbly knees, and heart palpitations. Such feelings are thought sacrosanct, and devotees think it positively sacrilegious to refer to them as mere "emotionalism."

Don't misunderstand me. I am thankful for this initial season of the marriage relationship. It is the magnet that brings two hearts together. It provides a jump-start to the matrimonial machinery. Unfortunately, it has its downside as well.

James Dobson tells a story of the football team from his mother's 1930 high school:

> It was located in a small Oklahoma town that had produced a series of terrible football teams. . . . Finally, a wealthy oil producer decided to take matters in his own hands. . . . This businessman proceeded to offer a brand new Ford to every boy on the team and to each coach if they would simply defeat their bitter rivals in the next game. . . . Finally, the big night arrived and the team assembled in the locker room. Excitement was at an unprecedented high. . . . They assembled on the sidelines, put their hands together and shouted a simultaneous "Rah!" Then they ran onto the field and were demolished, 38-0.[3]

All their emotions could not make up for a lack of discipline, training, experience, and character.

When a couple enters marriage on the momentum of feelings alone, their relationship is only as secure as their feelings. If *"the heart is deceitful above all things, and desperately wicked"* (Jer. 17:9), to build their future on such an unstable basis is to court disaster.

The feelings of romance are wonderful, but to fail to add discipline, training, experience, and commitment is a mistake. Emotions are wonderful, but to fail to add commitment and diligence in developing your relationship is to miss the blessing of growing through the seasons.

In the season of romance, effusive feelings blind a mate to faults. There is a tendency to idealize him or her, and to deny obvious flaws. If any quarrels occur, the couple makes up quickly and rarely comes to grips with the deeper issues. But time has a way of lifting the veil of romance to reveal . . .

Reality

One night shortly after my wife and I were married, I hung my dirty clothes on the bedpost. When I jumped into bed, Sandra asked, "Are you going to leave those clothes on the bedpost?" "No," I said, and dropped them on the floor. "Don't you think you should put them in the closet?" she asked patiently. "Why?" I wondered aloud. "The clothes are dirty and the floor is dirty. It's dark, so nobody can see them." "Because it's just neater," she countered, "and it's the right thing to do." The neater part I could argue with, but the declaration of right almost sounded righteous. I dutifully got out of bed and threw them into the closet and jumped into bed again. "Did you shut the closet door?" she inquired. "Honey," I said as I reasoned with her, "can you tell if the door is shut?" But by now I knew it was a losing battle. My days of carefree bachelorhood and unimpeded messiness were over. I realized that I had married a neat freak and Sandra realized she had married the master of disaster. Of course, she was right, and I needed her touch in my life. She had merely revealed a part of me that I had not seen or had happily ignored.

But having said that (in what I'm sure you will agree was a very humble tone), I hasten to add that it is vitally important to confess sins, so I feel a need to confess my wife's sin. You see, my otherwise sophisticated wife had a fatal flaw—she left the cap off the toothpaste. This would create a hardened plug of gritty toothpaste that defied the strength of Samson. I thought of placing the tube on the floor and stomping on it but feared the next day's newspaper headlines would read "Postman Killed by Flying Object of Unknown Origin!" I imagined the emergency room surgeon removing a plug of toothpaste and the hospital lab stymied as to its nature.

Small slights and disappointments—a forgotten anniversary, a facial expression, a gesture or unkind tone of voice—break the illusion of perpetual bliss. Compelling needs from childhood, well hidden under the veil of romance, now come forth in raw adult paroxysms: "You're just like your mother." "You work all the time. You're never home." "We just don't communicate."

But just when you wonder what you ever saw in this person, new life is breathed into the marriage with the arrival of a beautiful bouncing baby. All differences are forgotten in the glow of parenthood. Time-outs are called for all personality differences . . . for a while anyway. Then demands of parenting crowd out time alone. Financial pressures, work demands, and in-law relationships can further tarnish this idyllic picture.

It is during the season of reality that the seeds of small differences and misunderstandings are planted to later bring forth the trees of full-blown bitterness. *"Looking diligently lest any man fail of the grace of God; lest any root of bitterness springing up trouble you, and thereby many be defiled"* (Heb. 12:15). When these small resentments and disappointments are not dealt with in open communication and spiritual forgiveness, the natural result is . . .

REGRESSION

This season of regression is often accompanied by the advent of teenager-induced parenting conflicts, midlife crises, full-scale resentment, and entrenched bitternesses. Such unpleasantries often foster a loss of hope for the relationship and fantasies of escaping the pain. The ugly specter of divorce, while once unthinkable, often appears on the horizon and now becomes a frequent companion of your thoughts, even finding its way out in the open during tense discussions with your mate. While the majority of marriages take place during some phase of the romance season, the majority of divorces occur during the regression season. It seems that many who are at this point seek out someone who loves them as much as they love themselves and unknowingly begin the cycle all over again. While 50 percent of new marriages end in divorce, 60 percent of second marriages, and 70 percent of third marriages also fail.

Gone is the glow of romance with all its amenities of luxurious feelings. Those who don't understand the progression of the seasons dream of better days or even future options rather than work on present needs. Wives soak up frothy soap operas or lose themselves in romance novels in a desperate attempt to recapture the "romance." Husbands seek fulfillment in their work or sports. Some even fall prey to the temptation of an affair in the hopes of recapturing those ever-elusive feelings with someone else since they have "fallen out of love" with their mate.

This season of regression is most discouraging, and it is when many couples are tempted to give up. But hold on . . . it gets better!

REKINDLING

This season of rekindling is the result of a Spirit-empowered revival! This type of spiritual love and commitment is not the result of feel-good marriage seminars. It does not come from feeble attempts to work up the old feelings. It comes from God and it is all His doing. *"And the Lord make you to increase and abound in love one toward another"* (I Thess. 3:12).

It matters not where you are in the cycle of the seasons; anyone can experience this supernatural work of God. Even if you find yourselves in the pit of the regression stage, there is still hope. God can and *will* make your love to abound like never before!

While many things may be needed for this change in your life, not the least of which is good Bible teaching and biblical counseling, the most basic ingredient you will need is a sacrificial, raw-boned commitment to see it happen. The common denominator of victorious marriages is not effusive emotions or even common interests. It is not even the highly touted goal of compatibility. It is more a do-or-die commitment to the marriage than anything else.

The testing of any commitment is experienced not during the good times, the enjoyable season of romance, but rather during the seasons of disappointment. These seasons are to be expected, and your response to them when they come will make all the difference.

When our counselees are about to leave our program and return to what one of them called "the real world," we equip them with an understanding of the "death of a vision" concept. This is the teaching that in all spiritual goals, there are predictable stages of growth. When God gives a vision for good, it too goes through stages: first is the birth of the vision, then its death, followed by its rebirth. God told Abraham he would be the father of a great nation and his vision was born. Abraham and his wife Sarah grew old together without ever seeing a child born to them. Their vision had died. Then Sarah got pregnant with Isaac . . . vision reborn.

Spiritual growth is not charted as one straight line, heading northeast off the page. Rather, it is a very jagged line looking something like this:

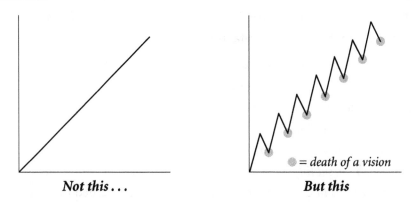

Not this...   **But this**

Progress is often interrupted, but the key is that the overall effect be one of upward growth and victory. That will depend upon your response to the occasional death of a vision represented by the low points on the graph. If you have a firm commitment to see your way through to God's ultimate purpose for your marriage, you will experience this growth. If you opt to bail out each time the death of a vision comes, you will not experience the joy of its rebirth. By forging an unshakable resolve and committing yourself unreservedly to your marriage "for better, for worse" and "'til death do us part," you will take a major step toward experiencing God's blessing on your union.

MYTH 2

COMPLICATED PROBLEMS HAVE EASY SOLUTIONS

It is commonly believed in Christian circles that it is easy to cure difficult problems of life (especially someone else's problems). Self-appointed therapists dispense flippant spiritualisms, which often cause more pain than healing.

Such advice as "Pray about it, brother!" to the speaker seems to swell with godly wisdom and authority, but to the aching heart who has prayed about it rings hollow. "Read your Bible, sister" likewise is good advice but a path worn bare from frequent use. Another approach is to encourage the discouraged to "get out and go soulwinning, brother. You need to get your mind off yourself!" Many of the pastors and missionaries I counsel at the Moorehead Manor have done just that—intensely and for years—but it doesn't resolve their marital problems.

You say, "But wait a minute here! Isn't it true that 'Christ is the answer'? So the solution is simple then, right?" It is true that Christ is the answer and it is true that biblical solutions are known for their simplicity. In fact, the apostle Paul writes to the Corinthian Christians about his concern for them: *"But I fear, lest by any means, as the serpent beguiled Eve through his subtilty, so your minds should be corrupted from the simplicity that is in Christ"* (II Cor. 11:3). Paul was concerned that the wisdom of the world would distract his converts from their simple faith in Christ. This was a legitimate concern then and it is a legitimate concern today. Christians by the scores have bought into mutant forms of "Christian psychology" because the complexities are strangely appealing.

Paul's argument is that the ultimate solution "in Christ" is simple. He is our source of wisdom. *"In Him"* is the place to find the answer for all of life's problems.

The problem comes when we confuse the *solution* of problems with the *resolution* of problems. Although Christ is the solution, to many people He is far off and out of reach. He is so far away that it is a cause of discouragement to hear others speak casually of His answers. They know He is the answer, but they also know that they don't have a clue as to how to get to Him. The steps of resolution from where they are to where He is are many and steep. They have already stumbled and fallen on more than one of them. They have learned that *"we must through much tribulation enter into the kingdom of God"* (Acts 14:22). It is in their tribulation that they languish. They need someone to take them by the hand and to say, *"This is the way. Walk ye in it"* (Isa. 30:21). Sometimes it is not so much a matter of "what" but "how."

A significant proportion of our clients at the manor are Ph.D.s and Th.D.s. They have the facts of theology clearly in hand. They have studied them for years, defended them before hostile panels, and written complex papers and preached deep sermons. What they haven't learned in many cases is how to apply what they've learned. They have a head knowledge about God but they don't know God. They even work their fingers to the bone serving God, but they miss a true intimacy with Him. Isaiah writes of this phenomenon: *"Wherefore the Lord said, Forasmuch as this people draw near me with their mouth, and with their lips do honour me, but have removed their heart far from me, and their fear toward me is taught by the precept of men"* (Isa. 29:13). This is not without a price: *"Therefore, behold, I will proceed to do a marvellous work among this people, even a marvellous work and a wonder: for the wisdom of their wise men shall perish, and the understanding of their prudent men shall be hid"* (v. 14).

What a sad picture. God's people had become busy-handed, empty-hearted, full-headed Christians. But their choice to remove their hearts from God had brought a curse: God would remove their wisdom and understanding. When Christians in the church pride themselves on their knowledge about God while failing to know God, the curse is still active. When Christian marriages have a *"form of godliness, but [deny] the power thereof,"* they fail to find the wisdom they need.

It is at this point that the enemy persuades learned believers that this is a simple matter and can be handled in-house. It is not really necessary to enlist a counselor. You know as much as he does. Take care of it yourself.

The solution is simple, but it is not always easily seen. Between the blindness, which comes from Satan, the wisdom that is removed by God, and the ascending steps of difficult circumstances and painful emotions, the resolution can be very difficult indeed.

If you find yourself at the point that you are in conflict because you've always believed that your problem is no big deal and should be easily resolved, but at the same time are struggling with overwhelming problems, perhaps it's time to seek help. A wise pastor, a spiritual friend, or a biblical counselor may be just what the doctor ordered. You may need someone to help you find your way to Christ, someone to point out the steps of resolution.

MYTH 3

IT'S NOT MY FAULT

A common experience for a marriage counselor is to encounter the time-tested practice of blaming others for personal problems. This is seen primarily in blaming the mate. A favorite reason for seeking marriage counseling in the first place is to position a wayward mate so that the counselor can change him. After all, the bulk of the marriage problems is the mate's fault. This has been the history of marriages from the very beginning. When God confronted Adam for his sin, Adam responded, "It's not my fault, it's the woman you gave me!" Eve responded, "It's not my fault. It's the snake's." And he didn't have a leg to stand on. And neither does the blame-shifting mate.

In a weak concession to this truth most mates will admit that a percentage of the problem is theirs (a very small percentage), but the majority definitely is thrown in the lap of the other.

UNRESOLVED GUILT

There is a delicate scale in the spirit of mankind that is akin to the old butcher's scale: a small dish on two sides. On one side would be placed a standard weight and on the other the portion of meat to be weighed. When the scale was level, the person weighing the material knew the weight and was paid accordingly.

It is of utmost importance for the scale of the spirit to be in balance. To maintain a sense of equilibrium and harmony of mind, it must be right. When it gets out of balance, the spirit feels out of kilter or cattywompus. Man cannot live for long in this state so he longs for balance.

The spiritual scale has two dishes. When one outweighs the other, disharmony settles in. Picture a scale with one side labeled "guilt." When you sin, God pushes down on the guilt side of the scale. To compensate and establish parity, you now have two choices. First, the spiritual choice. When you are convicted of sin and you say, "I have sinned," and confess it, the pressure is off and the scale is back in balance. The more popular and carnal method is merely to push down on the other side. That response is called "blame." Pushing on the blame side when God is pushing on the guilt side has become the method of choice. In fact, the tendency to push on the blame side reveals something shocking about a person: the tendency to blame is in fact an indication of guilt. The person who blames is a person who has not handled his guilt correctly. *"Thou that judgest doest the same things"* (Rom. 2:1). The person most likely to demonstrate undue criticism is the person who harbors guilt over similar sin.

A fascinating account in John's gospel demonstrates this. Early one morning as Jesus was teaching a crowd of people, His class was interrupted by a commotion. Breaking through the people into the very presence of the Teacher were a group of agitated Pharisees and scribes. They were dragging a hapless woman who they claimed had been caught in the very act of adultery. They demanded to know what Jesus thought should be done to her and reminded Him that the law required she be stoned. He quietly responded, *"He that is without sin among you, let him first cast a stone at her"* (John 8:7). It wasn't lack of knowledge of her sin to which Christ appealed but the presence of purity in the accusers. In fact, some suggest that Jesus was requiring that they be without the same sin. A. C. Gaebelein writes,

> Were they guiltless, or had they also broken the commandment, "Thou shalt not commit adultery"? If there was one in that company who had not sinned in this line he might come to the front and cast the first stone at the woman. They all sneaked out. The eldest left first; they were convicted by their own conscience. If they were guilty of the same sin which the woman had committed, then they were under the same sentence of death for the same sin. . . . What a testimony this is to the moral condition of the Jewish people in the days of our Lord! These Scribes and Pharisees with their high profession and pretensions were guilty of the grossest sin.[4]

It is thought then that the judges truly did the same thing. A primary reason for finding fault in another is that there is guilt that must be compensated by blaming.

Depletion of the Holy Spirit

Another reason for finding fault is spiritual emptiness and coldness of heart. When a believer goes without God for one day, he knows it. When he goes two days, his family knows it. When he goes three days, the whole world knows it.

Look at this picture of a man paddling his canoe downriver. Hidden under the surface of the water are obstructing boulders.

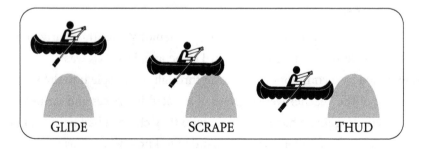

GLIDE   SCRAPE   THUD

The canoeist is the believer, the water represents the filling of the Holy Spirit, and the boulders represent the problems he sees in his mate. As long as the water level is high, the canoe glides over the boulder. When the filling of the Spirit is high, nothing seems to bother the believer. *"Great peace have they which love thy law: and nothing shall offend them"* (Ps. 119:165). He thinks the best of his mate, and personality quirks seem insignificant and harmless. He is living out the "Doctrine of the Glide."

But when he goes a day without God, the water recedes. The longer he is without God, the lower the water drops. Once the level has dropped enough, the canoe begins scraping the boulder. What didn't bother a marriage partner about his mate before now begins to irritate him slightly. This is the "Doctrine of the Scrape." Now the idiosyncrasies and peculiarities of the other's personality become a small annoyance and nuisance—small, but still annoying.

Then the level of the Spirit becomes so low that the boulder is looming high over the canoeist. It's in his face and cannot be avoided. He bangs into it over and over, wishing it weren't in his way and blaming it for interrupting his happy journey. This is the "Doctrine of the Thud." The things that were once unnoticeable, then annoying, have become a major source of irritation. It is at this point that the weary canoeist concludes, "The whole problem is the boulder!" And the marriage partner concludes, "The whole problem is my mate!" It never occurs to him that the level of the Spirit has diminished, only that the problem has gotten bigger. The Spirit is no longer in control; the flesh is. Because one mate does not walk in the Spirit, he tends to fulfill the lusts of the flesh. And the flesh says, "Your mate is your problem." That is interpreted to mean, "I must change my mate" or "I must remove my mate" rather than "I must seek the filling of the Holy Spirit."

THE "ACCUSER OF THE BRETHREN"

The enemy of your soul whispers to you that you're sleeping with the enemy. That's the real problem. He says, "You need to trade the old mate in for a new model . . . or a model! Then you would really be happy!" He says, "You didn't get married for all this pain. You need out!"

The entire focus has been centered on the mate. Naturally then, changing your mate becomes a priority. But your mate resists such efforts. And you persist. A wrestling match of sorts ensues, but Paul warns you to be sure that you're wrestling the right person: *"For we wrestle not against flesh and blood"*—this means that your mate really isn't the enemy after all—*"but against principalities, against powers, against the rulers of the darkness of this world"* (Eph. 6:12). Satan is the enemy. You've been fighting the wrong person!

How do marriage partners ever get to the place that they genuinely believe that their mate is the source of their problems? Satan is a master tactician, the supreme prosecuting attorney, and subtle in his attacks. He is called *"the accuser of the brethren"* (Rev. 12:10). In other words, he blames and accuses.

The word for accuser is *kategoros* from which we get the English words "category" and "categorize." As Satan accuses and blames your mate to you, you begin to think of him or her in categories. "You're just like your mother!" "Well, you're just like your father!" "You never . . . " "You always . . ." These blaming, accusatory, categorizing words create thoughts, which construct mindsets, which harden into belief systems, which ultimately come between you and the truth of God's Word as well as you and your mate.

Now that the enemy has accomplished his diabolical deed, he stands in the shadows and claps his bony hands together. He has accomplished the ultimate coup de grace: while he has been manipulating your thoughts, pulling the strings of your emotions, and making you angry, planting accusatory thoughts about your mate, he has hidden his role in the entire messy process. To make matters worse, he has convinced you that it's all your mate's fault. What irony!

BLAMING THE PAST

Another reason the "It's not my fault" myth is embraced is the practice of blaming current emotional and spiritual struggles on past traumas. Children who have been abused, neglected, abandoned, molested, and generally victimized by tragic childhoods eventually grow up and marry. Sadly, they often carry the emotional baggage from their past into their marriage. Abused children become dysfunctional teens who become psychologized adults. They are taught that their past traumas are the cause of their current personal struggles and that they can hope for nothing better than learning to live with these handicaps.

It becomes incumbent upon their mate then to accept them as they are and expect nothing more than a survival mode mentality. When problems arise, the past is blamed, parents are the culprit, and a less-than-understanding mate becomes part of the problem. It is no longer just the fault of the parents, but the insensitive mate as well.

This belief is traceable to a philosophy called determinism, which concludes that a person is determined to be the way he is by factors beyond his control. It might better be called "pre-determinism" since it is seen as determining one's behavior before it occurs.

Now there is no question that a painful past can have a negative influence just as a healthy past can have a positive influence. But the past is just that and no more: an influence. To confuse an influence with a cause is to embrace a worldview that says that "nothing is my fault; it's because of someone else," and eventually that "someone else" may be the person you've married. God destroys this notion in Ezekiel 18, when He demonstrates that a bad child can come from a good home and a good child can come from a bad home. It's all a matter of personal choice. Choice, not the other person in the relationship, is the ultimate cause of most relationship problems despite the influence that person carries.

No matter what the monsters of the past may be then, the believer can take heart in the fact that their influence is limited. They are limited in intensity because God *"will not suffer you to be tempted above that ye are able*" (I Cor. 10:13), they are limited in influence because any generation can "*see all his father's sins which he hath done, and [consider] and [do] not such like*" (Ezek. 18:14), and they are limited in duration because "*if any man be in Christ . . . old things are passed away; behold, all things are become new*" (II Cor. 5:17). Whatever the monsters in your past, their power is canceled at the moment of salvation by the power of the cross.

You can use your background as an excuse for present behavior only until you receive Jesus Christ as your personal Lord and Savior. After that you have a new power within you that is able to change your conduct. You have the Holy Spirit to empower you, the Word of God to guide you, the church to encourage you, the pastor to teach you, and prayer to connect you to God.

The Lord Jesus Christ concludes this discussion of "it's not my fault" by focusing on personal responsibility rather than blame shifting.

> "*Why beholdest thou the [splinter] that is in thy brother's eye, but considerest not the [log] that is in thine own eye? Or how wilt thou say to thy brother, Let me pull out the [splinter] out of thine eye; and, behold, a [log] is in thine own eye? Thou hypocrite, first cast out the [log] out of thine own eye; and then shalt thou see clearly to cast out the [splinter] out of thy brother's eye*" (Matt. 7:3–5).

It is clear from Christ's words that the person with the log in his eye is prone to go splinter hunting. A log is nothing but a bunch of splinters compacted together in one place. If you have a log in your eye, you have to look through it to see. If you do this, guess what you will see everywhere you look? Splinters! Your splinters! Have you ever met a person you didn't like and didn't know why until you figured out that he reminded you of yourself? The person with guilt projects it on others, especially in times of stress. "*Thou that judgest doest the same things.*"

The person with the log in his eye has to remove it before trying to remove a splinter from a brother's eye. Nobody wants a half-blind eye surgeon operating on him. Christ taught that one should make it a priority of purifying his own heart before attempting to purify another's.

It is tempting to embrace this myth. It's so comforting to think that someone else is to blame for the problems in your marriage. And this is not to deny any culpability on your mate's part. He may indeed be part of the problem. But the focus of Scripture is always your responsibility, not your mate's. The habit may be hard to break due to reinforcement over years of blaming, but it is a necessary step toward experiencing the spiritual revival God desires for your heart and your home.

---

[1] Ken Abraham, *Unmasking the Myths of Marriage* (Tappan, N.J.: Fleming H. Revell, 1990), 16.

[2] Abraham, 16.

[3] James Dobson, *Romantic Love* (Ventura, Cal.: Regal Books, 1989), 9, 11.

[4] Arno Clemens Gaebelein, *The Gospel of John* (Wheaton, Ill.: Van Kampen Press, 1936), 156.

8

MORE MYTH-INFORMATION

MYTH 4

"LOVE IS ALL YOU NEED"

I am suggesting that love may not be all it's claimed to be when it comes to the enjoyment of marriage. I can hear the screams of protest: "How dare you! You have desecrated the idol of romance!" "You have attacked the high priestess of the religion of the heart!" "What do you mean by this intrusion into the temple of warm fuzzies?"

It helps to understand that there are two key beliefs about love that fuel marital discontent. I encounter this consistently in my marriage counseling. The first is that "love is a feeling," and the second is closely related—"love is the basis for marriage."

"But everybody knows that love is a feeling! That's what romance novels and movies are all about! The TV talk shows and the psychological experts all agree on this." (At this point, I could rest my case, but I want to avoid appearing cynical). When the world comes to a consensus on any subject, it is cause for concern. The Lord Jesus Christ warned, *"Woe unto you, when all men speak well of you! for so did their fathers to the false prophets"* (Luke 6:26). It seems that it is possible to make much of people and their message even when they are dead wrong.

For the Christian, to make much of the world's message about love can make a marriage not only wrong but also dead.

Before you assume that the essence of love is a feeling, maybe you should examine where that notion originated. Did you learn that from the Bible? Or did you learn it from the culture? Sure, it is popular with the world. It always has been and always will be because romance and its attendant feelings give a buzz, a jolt, a high that routine commitment and duty to righteousness can't compete with. But then, street drugs give a buzz, a jolt, and a high that a good balanced diet can't compete with either. In time though, drug dependency can kill you. Maybe "dependency" on the drug called "romantic feelings" can do more damage than you think possible as well.

I have seen that damage firsthand; I have seen men leave their ministries, mothers leave their children, and Christians leave their God for the elusive high of romance. I have seen sin excused and the Bible traded like a comic book for the pleasures of "falling in love" with a stranger. I have seen inconsolable children whose hearts are broken, weeping in despair and dejection because daddy or mommy doesn't care about them anymore. He or she has found a new drug dealer. Believe me, I have witnessed enough heartache caused by this monster of romance to disregard the screams of protest about my views.

It is high time that somebody stand up and tell the truth on this subject! As a marriage counselor who has spent thousands of hours catching the tears and hearing the cries of broken-hearted marriage partners, I think I have a reason for doing so. The myth that love is all you need is dangerous and yet probably the most popular myth encountered in troubled marriages.

If love is a feeling and love is the basis for marriage, that translates logically into a conviction that feelings are the basis for marriage. This means then that when feelings disappear or dry up, so does any commitment. Why do people divorce today? People divorce because of feelings; either the romance has waned or departed, feelings of anger and hatred have displaced them, or both. But divorce has more to do with feelings than commitment.

And who says that love is the basis for marriage? Where did that notion come from? I once raised this question in a marriage seminar and a man tried to answer by pointing out that even the Bible teaches that a husband should love his wife. "Yes," I agreed, "but if he is a husband, he's already married." So then maybe marriage is more a basis for love than love is a basis for marriage. God's Word teaches that the husband should love his wife and the wife should be taught to love her husband and her children (Titus 2:4). God seems to be saying, "Now that you are married, now that you have made this commitment, you need to learn how to love." The world, on the other hand, says, "First, fall into feelings over which you have no control, then depend on those feelings for the security of your marriage. If those feelings ever change, get outta there!" Quite a difference!

The apostle Paul prayed for the Christians in Thessalonica: *"The Lord make you to increase and abound in love one toward another"* (I Thess. 3:12). He seemed to believe that love was more of a spiritual gift from God than an emotional product of man. Truly, if *"the fruit of the Spirit is love"* (Gal. 5:22), it would seem he is right. God certainly answered his prayer because in his next letter to these same Christians, he writes, *"We are bound to thank God always for you, brethren, . . . because . . . the charity of every one of you all toward each other aboundeth"* (II Thess. 1:3). Wow! No love songs needed! No touchy-feely seminars attended! No romance novels or movies used to work up a feeling! Just prayer! Old fashioned, simple, yet powerfully effective prayer! But behind every prayer is the God of prayer. It is not the formation of syllables, the shape of one's lips, or the noises uttered by a tongue that change things. It is the God to whom we appeal. Maybe it's time to discard the myth that "love is all you need" and trade it in for "God is all you need!"

Myth 5

"I Married the Wrong Person"

This intoxicating myth is one of the most common and dangerous of them all. It is the natural (or should I say carnal) result of disenchantment with your mate, which can lead to comparing him or her to the "one that got away."

"I Made a Mistake"

A wife is washing dishes with her arms buried in hot sudsy water while around the corner her husband reclines before a football game on TV. His face is covered with a stubbly beard, his hair is unkempt, and his T-shirt has crept up over his hairy belly. While he is indulging in a bag of chips, some of them fall onto his belly from which he disengages them while swigging down another soda pop.

This has no effect on her well-practiced habit of fantasizing about what could have been and ought to be. She is engrossed in selective memories of her high school sweetheart, who was tall and broad shouldered with a shock of black hair and blue eyes. As she is daydreaming of this Adonis, she recalls his name—Harry Hunk.

Suddenly her husband emits a belch. And she thinks to herself, "I could have married Harry Hunk but got stuck with Terry Twink instead. It's just not fair!"

A dutiful husband is cleaning out the attic for his wife when he stumbles across a trunk containing his high school yearbook. As he pores through its yellowed fungal pages, nostalgia sweeps over him. Then he sees her, Susie Sweetheart, his first love! Just like he remembers her— long blonde hair, soft blue eyes, and perfect complexion, and all in soft focus and back lighting to boot. He is transported into the land of "What If" when suddenly his reverie is shattered with the booming voice of his drill sergeant wife, "Have you taken the trash out yet!?" He thinks to himself, "I could have had Susie Sweetheart but ended up with Bella Barbell! It's just not fair!"

The conclusion? "I made a horrible mistake. I married the wrong person." How common this feeling of marrying wrongly is. In over a quarter century of marriage counseling, one of the most common complaints I hear is "I married the wrong person." A majority of married adults in my marriage counseling classes flirt with such thoughts. The result is untold suffering, including discouragement, bitterness, guilt, despair, and, sadly, even divorce.

Where does such thinking originate? Why do so many couples struggle with this myth?

I believe for some it starts in the teen years. Well-meaning youth pastors, pastors, and even parents warn teens that "God has just one person for you." This well-intentioned aim of putting fear into the mind of the young person and making him aware of the need to choose wisely can backfire. The teen often translates it as "Man, that means in all of the U.S. of A., Canada, Central America, South America, Europe, Greenland, the British Isles, and Australia, there is only one person for me. And I gotta go find 'em!" A rather daunting task, wouldn't you say? And what if he chooses wrongly? Eighty-one percent of Christian college students believe that "God selects one particular person for each person to marry," and 41 percent think, "Happiness in marriage is mainly dependent on marrying the right person."

If your mate is the basis of your happiness, if that mate fails to make you happy, or worse, starts causing you pain, you can easily conclude, "It is obvious what the problem is here; I got the wrong one!"

Dangerous Conclusions

The danger of the "God has only one person for you" philosophy is that there is a grievous misplacement of priority and focus. "Finding the right person" becomes all-consuming, while "being the right person" is minimized, if not ignored altogether. Some teens who are taught to make an itemized list of character qualities they desire in a future mate are not taught to develop their own character.

Second, this places all future happiness on a single decision—a lot for any endeavor. Even salvation, though it begins with a decision to trust Christ as Savior, doesn't end there. The initial decision is only the beginning. The process of spiritual growth involves many future decisions to follow God in various areas of life. The decision to marry a person is the beginning of a relationship, not the end. Many adjustments must be made in this relationship, and as each one is faced responsibly and with a firm reliance upon God, the marriage flourishes, despite the idiosyncrasies of a flawed marriage partner.

Third, it forgets that life presupposes change. In twenty years, nobody will be the same person in every regard that he is today. Life is bombarded with tests and trials and a variety of other pressures to which each person must respond. These countless variables have a cumulative impact on a person's character and personality. This is true for you as well as your mate. Time presupposes change, and the change may be for good or for bad. That's one reason the wedding vows of "for better or for worse" are so significant. You really can't predict what is ahead, but you can determine your commitment to see it through to the end.

Fourth, it ignores the selling of the product in the dating period. Let's face it—when you were dating, you wanted to make a good impression. Few people reveal all their fears, their character flaws, and their sins as a matter of course. We want our date to think the best of us, not the worst. A Catholic girl conspired with her mother to convince her Protestant boyfriend to turn Catholic so they could marry. The day before the wedding she burst into the house crying, "Mom, we oversold! He wants to be a priest!" There is a lot of overselling during the premarriage dating and courtship period.

Fifth, it denies your own personal responsibility in the marriage. To love your wife as Christ loves the church does not mean you are merely to love the lovely or the lovable. Christ died for sinners. Your responsibility to love your wife is dependent not upon the quality of her character but the quality of your love. To submit to a husband includes those that *"obey not the word"* (I Pet. 3:1), not merely those who are spiritually mature. Submission and trust are better measured in times of failure than times of success. If your husband is successful and sinless, how much trust is needed? It is your responsibility to trust God to work through your husband's failures. The husband has a responsibility to love, the wife has a responsibility to submit, and it is the responsibility that has to be embraced, not your right to happiness. To deny this with an inordinate focus on the making of a right choice is to miss the point and miss God's blessing as well.

Despite these things, many people still believe ardently that they married the wrong person. It may be related to the initial choice or other factors such as a choice to marry in violation of the parents' feelings, being unsaved at the time of the wedding, being married to an unsaved mate, or general unhappiness in the relationship. Whether the regret is traceable to a wrong choice of the past or unhappiness of the present, the result is a belief that "I married the wrong person."

But is it really possible to marry the wrong person? Is it possible that the person you're married to is really the right one after all? The answer to these questions will have tremendous repercussions, for good or for bad, in your marriage. It is tremendously important for you to do some ponderin' on this matter ("ponderin'" is a deeper level than thinkin'). To help you ponder, consider these facts.

Wrong Thinking About God

To believe that you're married to the wrong person gives tacit acceptance to the notion of living in a state of sin. If you began your marriage in sin, i.e., making a sinful choice, then you may conclude that you are perpetually living out the consequences of that sin. This is a state of sin with no means of correction and no closure. It is an open wound that defies healing. The question is whether that initial sin locks the couple into a perpetual, inescapable state of sin. While an act of sin can be confessed and forsaken, it is not possible for a state of sin to exist once the sin is put under the blood of Jesus Christ, which *"cleanseth us from all sin*" (I John 1:7). Even when the sin is so intensive and extensive that it abounds, the blood of Christ and the grace of God are greater. "*Where sin abounded, grace did much more abound*" (Rom. 5:20).

Many couples marry hastily for a variety of wrong reasons— gratification, obligation, lust, immaturity, and so forth. But even if the decision to marry was born out of the wrong motivation, indeed out of sin, it can be treated as a sin, confessed, and forgiven. On the other hand, to live with a sense of continuous guilt is not God's plan for anyone.

"GOD IS PUNISHING ME"

Upon inquiring of a wife her reasons for getting married, I asked, "Did you love your husband when you married?" "No," she replied. "Then why did you marry?" "We were promiscuous and we had to get married." I inquired further, "When you are alone with your thoughts and your husband comes to mind, how do you think of him?" Her shocking reply came immediately without hesitation. "I see my husband as an agent of punishment, assigned by God to purge me of my sins." Because she had begun wrongly, she thought that God was exacting a lifetime of punishment upon her through the pain of her marriage to achieve some form of atonement.

Sadly, this sentiment has been expressed often in counseling with slight variations. The conclusion is "Since I made a sinful decision, God is punishing me through this unhappy marriage." Since divorce is not an option, and happiness is out of the question, a mate must endure misery for the rest of his natural life. This is taking the old adage "Marry in haste, repent in leisure" to new heights.

With many life-changing decisions there is a natural time of uncertainty or doubt. Once, after I had signed a mortgage for a house, a friend asked me, "Have you had buyer's remorse yet?" I wasn't even aware there was such a thing, but it certainly makes sense. When you make such a major commitment, it is easy to wonder if you have done the right thing. The same is true in marriage; when doubts about marriage turn to fears and fears to regrets, a form of buyer's remorse may be the malady.

"IT'S ALL GOD'S FAULT"

There is another option: you can blame God. After all, you prayed for the right person, didn't you? You even sought godly counsel. Right? You trusted God to bring that special someone into your life, didn't you? Then what happened? God must have let you down. Of course, such sentiments will probably never be expressed consciously, but they slink around the edges of your consciousness, gnawing away at any remaining joy you might have in your spirit.

"GOD CAN'T BRING GOOD OUT OF EVIL"

One of the most overlooked qualities of God is His power to bring good out of evil. He delights in taking people from inauspicious beginnings to a grand and glorious finish! Joseph's life is one example of this. *"Ye thought evil against me; but God meant it for good"* (Gen. 50:20).

David's marriage to Bathsheba is another example of this. If ever there was a marriage that began wrongly, this is it. Born out of lust, adultery, murder, and deception, it is the poster child of everything that could be wrong about starting a relationship. If ever there was a marriage that should have failed, it's this one. If ever there was a union that should have been abandoned by God, this is it!

Yet, strangely, God chose to crown this union with exceptional blessings. He even chose this couple, of all couples, to bring the long anticipated Messiah into the world through their descendants. And He did so with gusto! He left nothing to guesswork or speculation. He records His choice boldly in Scripture, first in the gospel of Matthew, then Luke.

To satisfy the requirements of the Jews in qualifying the validity of any claim to messiahship, two things were necessary. First, the Messiah had to fit the legal qualifications represented by his father's sterling pedigree. The establishment of this required a thoroughly documented ancestry back to King David. This documentation of Joseph is found in Matthew 1. There, in the legal lineage of the Messiah, it is clear that the "father" of Christ is traced back to David. In the midst of this genealogy there is an anomaly; amidst all these "begats" appears this declaration: *"And David the king begat Solomon of her that had been the wife of Urias"* (Matt. 1:6). God is making a clear point here; in the tracing of Joseph back to Solomon and through Solomon to David, He underscores David's marriage to Bathsheba, the *"wife of Urias."* In doing so, He establishes Joseph's right to be the father of the Messiah, and in the process reminds the reader of David's sin.

Second, it was necessary to trace the Messiah's physical connection to King David as well. In Luke 3 we have the history that traces Mary's ancestry back to David. In verse 31 we find these words, *"which was the son of Nathan, which was the son of David."* Just as Joseph's ancestor was David, so was Mary's.

Here is where it gets interesting; we know who Solomon's mother was, but few people know that Solomon and Nathan had the same mother . . . Bathsheba![2] The legal and physical credentials of the Messiah are traceable to the marriage of David and Bathsheba.

Why this marriage? Why this wife of all David's wives to bring forth the Holy One of Israel?

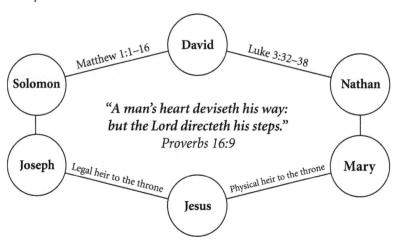

God is giving us a profound lesson on His ability to bring good out of evil. A marriage that began for all the wrong reasons ultimately was God's instrument for the greatest good ever given to mankind! It is true that David and Bathsheba began wrongly, but *"better is the end of a thing than the beginning thereof"* (Eccles. 7:8). Granted, David's heart planned it all out, but God was in control all the time. *"A man's heart deviseth his way: but the Lord directeth his steps"* (Prov. 16:9).

Even if your marriage began in the most evil of circumstances, even if you never gave a thought to God's role, even if you chose poorly or began sinfully, God never made a mistake! You are married to the right person. God meant it for good. The Lord has directed your steps all the way.

Maybe you didn't marry for the right reasons, but whomever you married is the right person for you. God wants to show the world how He can receive glory from a shaky beginning. He wants to demonstrate His power to merge two disparate personalities, literal "opposites," into one unified whole. He desires to apply His resurrection power to love turned stale and hearts turned cold. He wants you to treat your mate like the "right one after all."

---

[1] Steve and Annie Chapman, *Married Lovers, Married Friends* (Minneapolis: Bethany, 1989), 32-33.

[2] Orville J. Nave, "Nathan," *Naves' Topical Bible* (Nashville: Southwestern Company, 1962), 896.

9

FIVE FIBS ABOUT FALLING INTO FEELINGS

During the Vietnam War a young soldier stepped on a land mine that ripped both legs and one arm from his body. While lying in his own blood, he was hit by friendly napalm, severely burning him. I learned of him from a friend who had witnessed his last hours in a Tokyo hospital. The soldier's greatest fear was not facing life as a cripple or even the pain of surgery and rehabilitation but how this would affect his upcoming marriage. Unaware of the full extent of his injuries, his fiancée made her way to Tokyo. He feared her arrival, imagining the worst. When she walked into his room and saw a stump of a man with only one arm, a charred, blackened face, and a swollen head, she stood in silent shock. Without saying a word, she removed her engagement ring, placed it on the foot of his bed, spun on her heels, and strode out of the room and out of his life. For twenty-four hours he said nothing, weeping constantly. Then he died. His death, said the doctors, was not from his wounds but from his will. He no longer desired to live and simply gave up. He died from a broken heart.

Like many couples at some point in their relationship, this couple faced a crisis; they had to compete with the disillusionment of imperfection in the other. Sadly, more couples are losers than winners in this confrontation.

The most common complaint I hear in my marriage counseling is "We don't love each other any more!" And the most common question?

"How can we love each other like we used to?" For many Christian couples today, the uppermost thing in their mind is the revival of the love in their marriage. They hunger for something better, something deeper than they have.

There are several reasons for this love hunger, not the least of which is a misunderstanding about what lies ahead of them at the time of their wedding. Most couples naively enter marriage in a culturally induced state of emotional euphoria, which they fully expect to last forever. In fact, 78 percent of engaged youth fully believe that they are different from their predecessors or their parents. "We will never divorce!" they emphatically exclaim. "We are in love." Despite such protestations, 60 percent of new marriages are ending in dissolution—50 percent by divorce, 10 percent by separation. One of the leading reasons of such failures is an unholy yearning for self-centered emotional gratification.

A revival of love cannot take place if there exists a misdirected effort to satisfy a spiritual need in a carnal way. And usually, this is descriptive of dying marriages. With motivations born out of romance novels rather than the Bible, well-meaning Christians slavishly follow their worldly counterparts in lapping up the vile swill of the world's sewers instead of drinking at the fountain of living water. Such drugs of the heart are powerful, and there is no end to the number of dealers willing to provide them from their bottomless supply.

Addicts of such illegitimate highs often become incapable of distinguishing fantasy from reality. They gradually confuse the counterfeit for the real thing. And how can one be expected to go for the gold when he can't distinguish it from fool's gold? If unfulfilled expectations bring discouragement and depression, then it is vital that the differences in false love and true love be identified.

To help you in this process, this chapter will identify and isolate five dangerous, well-known lies about love. This is the *rooting out* and *pulling down* phase mentioned in chapter 7. In chapters to follow, we will build and plant.

Fib 1: Love Is Natural

"What?" I can almost hear the protestations at the suggestion of such an unpopular thought! "Of course love is natural. I know it is because I have felt it. How can you possibly say it's a fib that love is natural?" But if love were natural, why would God have to command the husband to do it?

Like the second law of thermodynamics, which teaches that any closed system left to itself will ultimately break down, so the natural inclination of the human heart is to degeneration. I call this tendency *"carnal gravitation."* In other words, there are identifiable areas in which humanity naturally gravitates downward. To identify these areas, one has to look no further than the commandments of God as He shores us up in our specific points of weakness. One of these areas is love, so He says bluntly, *"Husbands, love your wives"* (Eph. 5:25).

I once thought that such a command was not necessary for the wife due to her natural genteel nature and her feminine predisposition toward love and affection. As a youthful pastor, I even went so far as to say, "God commands the husband to love, but noticeable by its silence is any command to the wife to love. That's because of her natural, innate emotional makeup." A church member approached me after the sermon. "Pastor Binney," he said, "have you read Titus 2:4?" "No," I replied sheepishly. "But I think I'm fixin' to." Paul here admonishes the older women to *"teach the young women to . . . love their husbands, and* [amazingly] *to love their children"*! Apparently, mankind is incapable of sustaining love without some outside help. John reveals an essential source of this help when he writes, *"And this commandment have we from him, That he who loveth God love his brother also"* (I John 4:21). Do you see it? The husband is commanded to love the wife, the wife needs to be taught to love her family, and all believers are commanded to love each other. Why is all this necessary if love is natural?

FIB 2: LOVE IS PERPETUAL

That love is perpetual is a fib because love simply will not last on its own energy. Why? Because it has a natural enemy: *"And because iniquity shall abound, the love of many shall wax cold"* (Matt. 24:12). Remember the second law of thermodynamics? Any system left to itself will eventually deteriorate.

I was driving a car down the road when I noticed a clanging noise under the hood. The noise increased and I had barely pulled off the road when the car ground to a halt. Upon inspection I learned that the engine had literally seized up. The reason? I had neglected to put any oil in it, and it eventually broke down. The second law of thermodynamics had been activated. In my ignorance, I had failed to check the oil level. Sounds silly, doesn't it? But it's just as foolish for young lovers to assume that their love will keep on going. Most young couples fail to check the oil gauge of their marriage. I learned an expensive lesson; but while a car can be replaced, it's not as simple with a marriage partner.

While I was pastoring in Michigan, my wife, Sandra, and I spent an afternoon cross-country skiing. Upon our arrival back to our yard, we began frolicking like a couple of teenagers, rolling in the snow, kicking up our heels (all the time praying that no deacons would drive by), and I decided to kiss her. But the strangest thing happened. I made contact and even sensed pressure but experienced no feelings in my lips. Why? The prolonged exposure to the cold had constricted the capillaries that deliver blood to the surface of the skin. Gone was the source that warmed its surface and sensitized its nerves. My lips had turned blue from the cold and all sensation was gone. Likewise, when sin enters one's life, it has a chilling, constricting effect upon the vessels that carry love from the heart of God to the heart of man. In short, man is cut off from God, the very source of life and all love. *"Your iniquities have separated between you and your God, and your sins have hid his face from you, that he will not hear"* (Isa. 59:2). Sin is the natural enemy of love, blocking access to God. Is love forever? Not according to the Scriptures, not if sin enters a heart or relationship.

Fib 3: Love Is Emotional

Don't misunderstand me when I identify the idea that love is emotional as a fib. I am not saying that there are not emotions attached to love, that feelings don't accompany romance; but as someone wisely said, "Feelings are the dividends that God pays on the investment of obedience." Dr. Bob Jones Sr. often said, "Happiness is stumbled upon in the pathway of duty." The problem with many today is that they major on feelings and minor on duty. They would define love *only* in terms of emotion. With all the emphasis on subjective self-gratification, this should not surprise us. We have for so long fixated on feelings that I suspect much of what passes for love today is not what it seems. Instead of being in love with a person, many are in love with a feeling. Once the object of their love stops producing those feelings, their interest in that object stops as well. We laugh at the revolving door romances of teenagers, but it is no laughing matter when the same pattern persists into the marriage experience.

One evidence of true love is that it *"endureth all things"* and *"never faileth"* (I Cor. 13:7–8). What many mistake as love is actually infatuation. I had my first date in grade school. I fell in love over a cherry Coke that I shared with my beloved, a doe-eyed beauty with dark tresses and an enchanting smile. I was smitten! I couldn't eat or sleep. I thought only of her. So intense were the emotions that I could think of little else but her. I lived to see her in class and to be with her on the playground. This was real love! The sky was awash with the effects of the roman candles going off in my head! The only problem was that just as the colors faded, and the ashes of spent powder fell to the ground and disappeared, so did my feelings for the girl. Was it love? Not according to the biblical standard. I learned little from this experience except to look for a repeat. During the ensuing years, I entered into dozens of similar intense relationships with the same disappointing results.

I often wonder about the shortness of the "love" experienced by many dating young people. If love never fails, why do their feelings fail?

Could it be that the feelings they call love are really not love at all, or at least not the love about which the Bible speaks?

FIB 4: LOVE IS CONDITIONAL

To understand this fib that love is conditional, you must be aware of the three categories of love: "because of" love, "if" love, and "in spite of" love.

"BECAUSE OF" LOVE

"Because of" love finds its basis in the object of love. This kind of love says, "I love you because you're so pretty" (an assertion that has done wonders for cosmetic sales) or "I love you because you're so handsome." The natural result of such love in the waning years of life is to fear the decline of youthful appearance, to doubt the depth of love of someone who would abandon you for a newer model, or to misplace emphasis on conserving a bebop attractiveness.

"IF" LOVE

The "if" love finds its energy not so much in the object of love but in the results of love. "I love you if you meet my needs, if you make me feel good, if you meet all my expectations!" This kind of love is totally dependent upon the performance of the other for happiness. The person with an "if" love is the slave of the object of his love. If his lover does well, he's happy; if she does poorly, he is unhappy. This is a miserable existence at best, but it is the lot of many married people today. Their self-centered view of love has chained them to an ideal they can never fully realize.

"IN SPITE OF" LOVE

The "in spite of" love is dependent upon neither the appearance of a mate nor the results of performance. This love transcends all other loves. It says, "I love you in spite of your scars, in spite of your weight, in spite of your failure, even in spite of your sin." This is the love of God, who said, *"I have loved thee with an everlasting love"* (Jer. 31:3). And this kind of love is available to every person who loves with God's love. It is not conditioned on appearance, perfection, or performance but on the love of God, which is *"shed abroad in our hearts by the Holy Ghost"* (Rom. 5:5). You, too, can enjoy this love. You must have this love if your marriage and other relationships are to prosper.

FIB 5: LOVE IS MEASURABLE

The acceptance of the fib that love is measurable is seen in the tendency of many people to view love as a finished product, no assembly or maintenance required. They enter marriage planning to sit back to enjoy a new-found toy, never suspecting that adjustments might have to be made, that some parts may require oiling, that some soap and polish are needed to maintain its luster.

When my son Jonathan was in grade school, he came to me and said, "Dad, I sure would like to have a dog." What boy wouldn't? "But son," I protested, "we can't have a dog. A dog has to be fed every day." "I'll feed him, Dad! He'll be the fattest dog in the neighborhood!" How can you argue with such devotion? "He has to be kept clean." "He can take a bath with me every night!" Oh, the commitment of this boy! I was weakening and fast losing ground in this discussion. "The most important thing," I intoned in my most parental voice, "is to clean up after the dog." I will spare you the details of the next promise this elicited from my son, who sensed a victory. Yep, you guessed it. I got him his dog, and I am proud to announce that he kept all his promises . . . for two weeks. It wasn't long before our new yellow lab pup was nosing an empty food dish around the kitchen, scratching vigorously, and . . . well, you get the picture. What had happened? My son had an idealistic view of doghood. He saw a dog as a leaping, licking, tail-wagging bundle of perpetual happiness—no care, feeding, or maintenance required—not unlike the view that many newly married couples bring to matrimony. It's not that they see their mate as a "dog," but neither do they see him or her as a commitment. Perhaps the truism "Puppy love can lead to a dog's life" has merit after all.

Like my young son, many marriage partners see love as a product and not a process, when in truth, love is a process and not a product. This is what Paul underscored when he wrote, *"And the Lord make you to increase and abound in love one toward another"* (I Thess. 3:12). The love he envisioned was not static but fluid, ever growing, ever increasing, ever abounding. He made no attempt to measure it because it was at an open-ended process: never ending, never complete, always improving.

Many couples enter marriage confident that all the work has already been done. After all, they are in love. Sure, some old fogeys have tried to warn them about the work ahead, but they are obviously too old to understand. Veteran marriages lack the pizzazz and the love they have. They feel light years ahead of stale marriages that they believe they can avoid. Can I make a confession? When I stood at the wedding altar watching my lovely bride glide to my side, my thoughts were not "Bless God, here comes a commitment!" They were more akin to "Hot diggety dog! Here comes a bundle of love that's gonna make me feel good!" Like my son, I saw a packaged product that required no assembly, maintenance, care, feeding, or cleaning. I did not understand that love is a process that requires constant attention and nurturing. Many marriages fail because of this basic lack of understanding.

If your marriage is to flourish, it must be based on truth rather than on error. Your conceptions of love must be based on something more solid than experiences, feelings, or popular cultural beliefs. You must base your future on the Word of God. Contrary to the claims of movie magic, *reel* love is not *real* love. You must understand love if you are to build a marriage and a family that will stand the test of time. The starting place is to identify any lies you have believed and then replace them with the truth of God's Word.

We have learned what love *isn't*. What is it? What does God say is biblical love? That is the subject of the next chapter.

10

NIBBLED GIZZARDS

A self-appointed youthful philosopher described love in this way.

Love is such a funny thing
It's something like a lizard
It worms its way into you
And nibbles at your gizzard.

Many people, it would seem, are motivated by the rush that the nibbled gizzard provides. For good or for bad, many relationships are based upon the feelings of the moment.

This was brought to my attention in a recent week of counseling. One godly man was bemoaning the fact that he was no longer "in love" with his mate, meaning there were no more feelings and that he had "fallen out of love."

Another couple's marriage was threatened because one mate had "fallen in love" with a third party and was prepared to abandon all family commitments for this new relationship. So here before me was one marriage about to break up because of a lack of feelings for a mate, and another marriage about to dissolve because of the presence of feelings for someone else.

This gave me pause to reflect on the various ways in which "love" impacts relationships.

THE MINISTRY OF MARRIAGE

THE LOVELORN

The lovelorn is the person who is deserted by or pining away for a sweetheart. The ultimate victim of unrequited love, the lovelorn has been the recipient of the infamous "Dear John" letter and is nursing a gaping wound of the heart. This emotional injury may have been inflicted by abandonment, by neglect, or by being ignored by the object of love; but the result is a heart-wrenching despair. The desperation of such people is vividly demonstrated by the reaction of a fifteen-year-old in Conyers, Georgia, who, distraught over his breakup with his girlfriend, went on a shooting spree, wounding six of his classmates.

THE LOVESICK

The lovesick is the person so desperately in "love" with another that he is rendered practically incapable of carrying on in a normal fashion. Most typically it is a person who is dating or engaged, consumed by thoughts of his lover. He cannot function without his daily (hourly?) fix of a glance, a touch, a word, or, most important, the presence of his beloved. He is addicted to a person and every moment apart he experiences "cold turkey" withdrawals until he can get his next dose.

THE LOVELESS

The poor loveless soul experiences the ultimate rejection, not that of breaking up with his lover but of never having had a lover in the first place. This may be an unmarried person frantic to find a mate for life but unable to connect with anyone. It may include the lonely teen who feels a total sense of isolation and rejection while all around friends gush over their latest romance. But it can also include that person who feels incapable of feeling any emotions at all. He questions his normalcy, even sanity because he is deprived of any surges of feelings whatsoever: anger, depression, joy, and especially love. This creates problems in marriage, especially when the ultimate measure of true love is reduced to feelings and feelings alone.

The Loveblind

The loveblind is blinded to any faults in the object of his love or to problems in the relationship clearly evident to everyone else. Others are blinded by the love that should not be: the relationship disallowed by culture, by morality, by others, and even by one's own previous standards. Yet they experience supercharged feelings that sweep all opposition and restraint away in their path. I have counseled brokenhearted husbands whose wives of many years and of consistent faithfulness have met someone in an Internet chat room, and they have inexplicably turned their backs on their children, their marriage, and even their ministries to leave town with a relative stranger, all in the name of "love." They have been blinded.

The Love Magnet

Less well-known but still someone to consider is the love magnet, one who is so beautiful, handsome, popular, talented, famous, or wealthy that he seems to attract suitors from every crevice, almost without effort. He has a gnawing fear that he is never really loved for himself. He wonders if it isn't what he represents that attracts others to him.

The Brain-dead

The inescapable conclusion is that America is drunk with "love." The glands have neutralized normal thought processes; the heart has overridden the mind. The brain is dead. It is no longer capable of clear, logical, or biblical reasoning. Man is out of control.

The church is not exempt. Christian teens and adults alike have sold out to their feelings. Dating relationships begin and end with feelings; marriages are born and quickly die because of them. Engagements are made in haste and just as quickly abandoned because of them. Former lovers become enemies, couples enter into addictive chain relationships from revolving-door dating patterns to multiple affairs, and on to repeated divorces based on little else than a weak "we don't love each other anymore" excuse (translated "we don't have the feelings we once had").

Love, it would seem, is a cruel and capricious goddess. Wounded spirits by the millions are left in her wake as people are discarded as "used goods." Jilted lovers react with bitterness; offenders are seen as the "enemy." Distrust is entrenched in the hearts of the wounded and lives are changed forever.

The natural question to ask in light of all this is "Why?" Why are so many so easily deceived by their emotions?

CULTURAL CONDITIONING

Let's face it! Our culture marches in a lock-step formation with this world. There is very little disagreement on what love is, what its role is, how to get it, how to lose it, and how to use it. Everyone is an expert in the field of love. Few would dare raise an objection to this overpowering consensus of the present world.

THE MEDIA

From romance novels to movies, from TV soap operas to sitcoms and talk shows, from country music to soft rock, our culture screams with one voice: "Love is all you need!" I was intrigued some years ago as I watched an interview of Burt Bacharach, at that time one of the most prolific songwriters of popular music. He was asked, "How do you come up with ideas for all these songs you write?" "It's simple," he replied, "I just think of another way to say I love you."

THE DATING DILEMMA

Young people are conditioned heavily and prejudiced enormously by the dating process. The initial attraction begins with a feeling. It is a feeling that holds them together; and when the feeling stops, they drop the other to seek another source of emotional highs. They begin the process anew until the feelings stop and then they dump partner number two. This goes on until they finally find the "right one." Before the feelings have time to wane, they tie the knot; and in short order, like all the times before, the feelings stop. Almost habitually and out of conditioned response, they quickly assume that the diminished feelings mean that the marriage is over. After all, everyone knows that love is a feeling, and that love is the basis for marriage, right?

It stands to reason that this translates into "Feelings are the basis of marriage." To paraphrase the plaintive cry of many counselees: "Feelings are the glue that holds us together. As long as you provide me the feelings I need, I will stay with you. Happiness in marriage is dependent on finding the right person, and I thought you were the right person as long as you made me happy. But I'm not happy anymore. I didn't get married for this pain. I am going to resort to my dating pattern and dump you the moment you don't offer a return on my investment." And thus the conditional dating experience becomes the conditional marriage relationship.

OUTSIDE PRESSURES

The average person is under enormous pressure to conform to this widely popular conception of love. We have gone from a society that once promoted courtship, strict chaperoning, and a minimum age requirement of sixteen to actually pressuring our preteen youth to "find a date." It is not uncommon now to see grade school children in dating relationships. As well meaning as the promotion of this may be, it is usually based on the concept that happiness is found in love. But when a young person asks what love is, he is often met with a condescending grin, a wink of the eye, and a patronizing "You'll know it when you feel it."

WEAK AND NONEXISTENT TEACHING ON LOVE

The current teachings about love add to the problem. Much preaching and teaching in the church about love never bother to thoroughly explain what is meant by the word. This sets up the listener to bring his own understanding of the word to the subject. And where did he get his understanding but from the world? The listener, then, is set up to embrace the lie through default.

Worse yet, some spiritual authorities even promote the idea of feeling-based love. Building upon the assumption that love is in fact an emotion, counselors make love a major prerequisite for happy relationships. Parents direct their children's thoughts about marriage with the all-important question "Do you love him?"

EMOTIONAL PROMISCUITY

One of the strengths of the church is her emphasis on sexual purity. From preteen years and up, there is a consistent emphasis on the need to keep the body for the marriage partner. Christians deplore the sin of sexual promiscuity, and so we should.

But less understood is the sin of emotional promiscuity. Just as we are to keep our body in subjection, we are to *"keep [our] heart with all diligence; for out of it are the issues of life"* (Prov. 4:23). The same self-control needed for the body is needed for the heart. Sexual promiscuity involves losing control of our body, letting our physical passions overwhelm us, and yielding to our body's demands for gratification. Emotional promiscuity involves losing control of our emotions, letting our feelings overwhelm us, and yielding to our heart's demand for gratification. The issue is the same. God is not in control; our passions are in control. Self is not in control; our emotions are in control. The will and the mind are not in control; the heart is in control. The spirit is not in control; the flesh is in control.

The danger of emotional promiscuity is greater than sexual promiscuity. Why do I say this?

IGNORANCE

While we are clearly aware of the dangers of sexual sin, we are deplorably ignorant of the effects of emotional surrender. The defenses we have so carefully erected for sexual temptation do not exist for emotional temptation. We cannot *"resist the devil"* if we are *"ignorant of his devices."*

The Deceitful Nature of the Heart

We do not understand that the nature of the heart is to be wicked and to fool us: *"The heart is deceitful above all things and desperately wicked: who can know it?"* (Jer. 17:9). Many do not realize this. Others refuse to acknowledge it. The best advice given by many humanists is "Trust your heart." The foolhardiness of such counsel should be apparent. But it gets worse.

Not only is the heart deceitful, it is *"deceitful above all things."* This is rather conclusive, don't you think? *"All things"* includes but is not limited to the mind and the will. But the message is clear: there is nothing, absolutely nothing, that will deceive you and mislead you more quickly or more thoroughly than your emotions. Period.

There is more. The heart is also *"wicked."* This is getting rather unsettling, isn't it? God has not only told us that our heart is deceitful, and deceitful above all things to boot, but He is also now telling us it is downright *"wicked."* Bad news indeed for the impulsive suitor who follows his heart. But wait! The verse continues; the heart is *"desperately wicked."* God's use of powerful modifiers here is to make an exceedingly strong case. The conclusion is inescapable; the heart is so deceitful and so wicked, nobody can ever fully understand it. It is so unpredictable and unstable you can't rely on it. The light of joy today is the blackness of despair tomorrow. Yesterday's elation of love becomes today's angst of anger.

If maturity is the ability to conform our beliefs to the Bible, the mature love will conform his heart to this powerful truth: he can't know his own heart. *"He that trusteth in his own heart is a fool"* (Prov. 28:26).

Your Sweetheart's Heart Can Deceive You

You can't know anyone else's heart either, especially that of the object of your love. The man in your bed may not be the man who stood beside you at the wedding altar. The woman at your table may be radically different from the girl you picked up for that first date. Your sweetheart's heart may turn out to be sour.

Your Sweetheart's Heart Deceives Him

Your lover can't understand his own heart. He may honestly express his depth of feeling without a clue that those feelings can ever change or that they are misleading him.

"Who can know it?" is the question of the ages. This universal inability to understand your heart includes motives, the conclusions formed by the heart, as well as the sources of its information.

I once heard the question posed about a president's foolish dalliances with a fickle intern: "Why would the most powerful man in the nation, the leader of the free world, risk everything on her?" There is no answer to the question because it presupposes that his head was in control rather than his heart. Sin has never been about logic but about emotions. The former president himself can't answer that question because he was deceived by his heart and under the control of emotions. He was compelled forward by a deceitfully wicked heart of which he had no comprehension. And so is every person whose "love" is dependent on any other source than God Himself.

Because of this, there is a certain amount of faith needed when venturing onto the sea of matrimony. It is a mistake to assume your heart will always be a bottomless fountain eternally bubbling with the effervescence of love.

Emotional Surrender Precedes Sexual Surrender

A danger of emotional promiscuity is that it usually precedes sexual promiscuity and sets up the participant for further compromises. Few cases of adultery in marriage are purely physical in origin. It is rare if not unknown for a person to be approached with a sexual proposition that is not conditioned by a gradual and lengthy emotional entanglement. By the time the actual sexual temptation is offered, the resistance has been broken down and the reasoning ability has been dulled by intense emotional euphoria. The person is defenseless: *"He that hath no rule over his own spirit is like a city that is broken down, and without walls"* (Prov. 25:28). In the days of this Scripture, the primary defense of a city was its walls. In the face of invaders, the inhabitants would flee to the city and close the gates. Naturally, if there were a breach in the wall, the enemy could easily gain entry. But to have no walls was unthinkable. A person who has no control over his emotions or his amorous passions is like a city without walls. The enemy marches in at will.

SATANIC DECEPTION

You do have an enemy! He is dangerous, destructive, and constantly seeking ways to destroy you: *"Be sober, be vigilant; because your adversary the devil, as a roaring lion, walketh about, seeking whom he may devour"* (I Pet. 5:8).

Make no bones about it; the Devil wants to get to you. One of his primary means of doing this is to "roar." Fortunately, we have identified that roar. Instead of approaching us through fear then, the Devil uses fascination; instead of fright, he uses fantasy; rather than roaring, he whispers. Instead of coming as a lion, he comes as a subtle serpent, even an angel of light: *"For Satan himself is transformed into an angel of light"* (II Cor. 11:14).

As an angel of light, he looks for the most vulnerable part of man through which he can gain access to his will and bring him into complete bondage. What is that part of man? It is the heart, the seat of emotion. This is his target and this is where his subtle control is most often manifested. And why? *"The heart is deceitful above all things, and desperately wicked: who can know it?"* (Jer. 17:9).

The record is clear; Satan has the power to deceive the whole world (Rev. 12:9; 13:13–15), he takes the world captive "at his will" (II Tim. 2:26), and he even fools many Christians (Matt. 24:24). How does he do this? He uses feelings of "love" to convince the unwary that all love is good, even godly: "it can't be wrong when it feels so right." He even goes so far as to use these feelings to recruit the ignorant into false cults, justify affairs with feelings of "love," rush the impressionable into premature marriages, and often give the discouraged an excuse for divorce.

Most notably, the Deceiver has the power to manipulate the feelings of the heart through *"wonders."* This is a key to understanding how he can fool the believer. Satan works *"with all power and signs and lying wonders."* (II Thess. 2:9). The word *"wonders"* mentioned here is different than the words *"mighty works"* and *"signs"* used elsewhere in Scripture. *"Mighty works"* has to do with the power and grandeur of the act, *"signs"* is related to the doer's supernatural power, but the significance of *"wonders"* is the effect it has as it awakens amazement within the spectator.[1] It is the emotion that it evokes within the observer in question here. It is excitement, surprise, amazement, awe, which causes one to admire another.[2] Do you get the picture? Satan is able to stir the emotions of mankind to the point that they will actually worship him as God. He has his own doctrines (*"doctrines of devils"*) his own messengers (*"seducing spirits," "ministers . . . transformed as the ministers of righteousness"* II Cor. 11:15), and his own medium (*"wonders"*). And he targets all this at man's weakest point, the heart, often through the influence of another person. "Three times [wonders] are ascribed to the work of Satan through human agents."[3]

It is the same Devil and the same power that can produce synthetic feelings of love in the heart of mankind today! If Satan can use human agents to evoke wonder toward him, can he not use a human agent to evoke your wonder toward another person? These feelings that cause one to admire another are the very foundation of infatuation, which we call "love." Satan has the power to produce these feelings, and he can accomplish this through other humans. If the truth were known, much of what passes for love is really a *"wonder."* How much of what we claim comes from God really originates from seducing spirits who bait us with feelings and deceive us with white-hot emotions? How many people have been misled into twisting the Scriptures, which say, *"God is love,"* to mean "love is God"? Is the world being conditioned to worship Satan through the habit of wondrous emotions? Have we played into his hands by prizing feelings as the ultimate attainment and elevating our hearts to the level of infallibility?

The Wrong Focus for Satisfaction

Many marriages are pining away because of a horrible disparity in the relationship. Each partner is looking to the other for fulfillment he can never give. For years each has been taught that there is only one person in the world and that finding the right person is the only guarantee of a happy marriage. Not realizing that being the right person is more important to lasting marital joy than finding the right person, mates naively set out to place an onerous burden upon the object of their love. Each looks to the other for fulfillment, happiness, and an endless supply of emotional warm fuzzies.

It is patently unfair, however, to place upon your mate a responsibility that no human is capable of achieving. Love, joy, and peace are not the "fruit of the spouse" but the "fruit of the Spirit." No human is capable of accomplishing what he was not designed to do.

Secondly, it is dangerous to the extreme to leave God out of the picture. Placing the burden of emotional happiness upon a human impugns the very purpose of God. He is to be our source of fulfillment, and He alone!

Even without the acceptance of another human being on this earth, I can be *"accepted in the beloved."* With nobody else to complete me I am still *"complete in him."* No person can provide my sufficiency because *"my sufficiency is of him."* To look to any other source but God for my sense of wholeness is futile and an invitation to disaster.

God is a jealous God and shares His glory with no one. He is looking over the battlements of heaven, desiring for you to look to Him for every need of your heart. To His dismay, He watches you looking around you instead of above you. He grieves as your heart is given almost totally to another finite sinner just like you. Now He is in a difficult position. If He blesses this godless effort, He condones an act of rebellion against Him and concedes to the lie that a man can take His place. He can't do that because He cannot share His glory with another. On the other hand, if He allows the relationship to struggle, His loving heart is grieved to watch you suffer in the process. But He has no choice. He watches in pain as you struggle through the valley of your relationship to discover that this person is not what you thought he would be and is incapable of providing the emotional fulfillment you need. After a period of suffering (which varies from person to person), you are jolted into the truth; only God can meet your needs. When you turn to God, experience His sufficiency and the filling of His Holy Spirit, the overflow of that relationship is enough to minister deeply to your mate. Without it, you can do nothing.

I am convinced that the reason God allows marriages to go through the seasons of disappointment is to remind the romantically deluded that He is the source of all the love they could ever desire. He wants to be your all in all. Yes, it's true that He works through one mate to meet the needs of the other to some degree, but He still desires your trust to be channeled through your mate to Him, and not around Him to your mate.

The ultimate reason that any person fails to enjoy the fullness of his God-designed capacity for boundless love is that he has looked to the wrong source for that love. Where are you looking?

CONCLUSION

The lovelorn, the lovesick, and the brain-dead will long be with us. Their preoccupation with nibbled gizzards will be their undoing. You may be among them unless you understand some of the causes for this terminal condition. Only by understanding them can you put them off and put on the truth. May God help you to do so.

---

[1] Kenneth S. Weust, *Philippians Through the Revelation* (Grand Rapids: Wm. B. Eerdmans Publishing Co., 1959), 62.

[2] E. W. Bullinger, *A Critical Lexicon and Concordance to the English and Greek New Testament* (London: Bagster and Sons, 1969), 895.

[3] W. E. Vine, *An Expository Dictionary of New Testament Words* (Westwood, N.J.: Fleming H. Revell Co., 1940), 228.

11

How to Grow Your Love

And the Lord make you to increase and abound in love one toward another, and toward all men, even as we do toward you: to the end he may stablish your hearts unblameable in holiness before God, even our Father, at the coming of our Lord Jesus Christ with all his saints.
I Thessalonians 3:12–13

While eating out with Sandra one evening, I observed two common extremes in marriage today. Across from us and oblivious to the world, was a young couple. Obviously newlyweds and probably on their honeymoon, they spent the entire meal looking deep into one another's eyes, whispering sweet nothings, holding hands, and occasionally, placing a bit of food in their mouth. It was a marvel of engineering that they could do that with everything else going on, but of course, eating was not a top priority for them anyway.

The other extreme was represented by an older couple in their midsixties, sitting only a few feet away from the young lovers. They were obviously seasoned veterans of the marital experience. They never looked at one another, never spoke, played in their food, and looked out the window.

The young lovers got up to leave. If it was a marvel that they could eat and do all this, you should have seen them walk and do it. With arms so tightly wrapped around one another you couldn't have gotten a human hair between them, and eyes locked on each other, they still managed to maneuver their way between the tables of the restaurant. He paused to open the door gallantly for his lady fair, and she floated through the door. He offered his arm for the treacherous journey across the parking lot, opened her car door, gingerly tucked her dress in, and softly closed the door. He hurried around to the driver's side and by the time he got there, she had scooted over under the wheel leaving him little room. He didn't mind, however, and they drove out of the parking lot, two heads merged as one.

Meanwhile, back at the table, the veteran couple were fed up, so they got up to leave also. He walked twenty feet in front of her. By the time she got to the door, it had slammed in her face, and by the time she got to the car, the brake lights were on and the engine running. As she was shutting the door, the car started moving. The car drove out of the parking lot with the husband on his side of the car and the wife on the far side. Sadly, between youthful love and veteran relationships, couples often find themselves drifting apart.

This does not have to be. It is God's will for your love to grow and your relationship to blossom. This is clear from the admonition of the apostle Paul at the beginning of this chapter. Take a moment to read it carefully. To whom is this great truth addressed? To you the reader! And when does it apply to you? Every time you read it. That means that from this moment God's plan and desire for you is to "increase and abound in your love." That's a love that is constantly expanding and developing!

In a previous chapter we discussed some of the reasons this fails to happen: reasons such as a failure to understand the natural and predictable seasons of a marriage and the culturally induced misconceptions of what love really is. Another reason that love fails to grow, however, is that we do not apply the biblical principles of growth that are needed. What are these principles?

BE SAVED

A foundational principle, which may seem basic to the Christian reader, is the need of being born again. But its importance cannot be overlooked. In the first place, it is a dangerous thing to miss this starting place of godly love, because one cannot love with godly love unless one is indwelt by the Spirit of God: *"For love is of God; and every one that loveth is born of God, and knoweth God. He that loveth not knoweth not God; for God is love"* (I John 4:7–8). God says that He is the origin of love and that one must know Him to experience such love. The apostle Peter confirms this. After writing of the need to *"love one another with a pure heart fervently,"* he added a qualifier: *"being born again"* (I Pet. 1:22–23). If to know God is to love and to love is to know God, when love is absent from a relationship, it is wise for the loveless to examine his relationship with God.

This is not an exercise in futility; it is always wise to *"examine yourselves, whether ye be in the faith"* (II Cor. 13:5). Why? Because Jesus warned that *"not every one that saith unto me, Lord, Lord, shall enter into the kingdom of heaven. . . . Many will say to me in that day, Lord, Lord, have we not prophesied in thy name? and in thy name have cast out devils? and in thy name done many wonderful works? And then will I profess unto them, I never knew you"* (Matt. 7:21–23). It is with good reason, then, that well-known church leaders estimate the number of lost church members to be as high as 50 percent! And it is with good reason that every marriage partner examine his own heart before God as to the state of his salvation. If love is absent, it is an indication that either one's relationship with God is nonexistent or his fellowship with God is weak. Either case is cause for alarm.

Be Spirit-Filled

Just as it is important to be indwelt by the Spirit of God in salvation, it is vital to be filled with the Spirit of God in your daily life. In Ephesians 5, Paul wrote, *"And be not drunk with wine . . . but be filled with the Spirit"* (v. 18) and placed this command strategically in the Scriptures to precede submitting to your husband and loving your wife (vv. 22, 25). Why? Because these things are not possible without being filled and energized by the Holy Spirit of God. If *"the fruit of the Spirit is love"* (Gal. 5:22), then the Spirit-filled wife will possess a loving submission to her husband and the husband will enjoy a true Spirit-empowered love for his wife. Both will be under the spiritual control of God.

These principles may seem basic to the initiated, but basics are important. One man said, "The main thing is to keep the main thing the main thing." I recall that at the beginning of every basketball season our coach required that we spend a day practicing our dribbling, another day our passing, and yet another our footwork before we shot the first ball at the hoop. When asked about this, he replied, "We've got to master the basics first." We've got to learn some basic spiritual truths about love because they are the "main thing."

PRAY FOR LOVE

Another of the basics often overlooked is what one counselee called a "novel approach" because he had not thought of it before. What was it? I had asked him, "Have you prayed for more love for your wife?" Then I asked him, "What if I could guarantee you that God would answer your prayer?" I showed him I John 5:14, *"And this is the confidence that we have in him, that, if we ask any thing according to his will, he heareth us."* "Is it God's will for you to love your wife?" Then I asked his wife, "Is it God's will for you to love your husband?" When they both responded yes, I said, "Then we can know that He hears us." I read verse 15, *"And if we know that he hears us, whatsoever we ask, we know that we have the petitions that we desired of him."* Notice God's progressive guarantee; if we ask according to His will, He hears us, and if He hears us, He answers us. The revival of love in many marriages is waiting on heart-motivated prayers to God to rekindle *agape* love. If it is true that *"ye have not, because ye ask not"* (James 4:2), then it remains only for the sincere to ask.

As you ask, however, be certain you're asking for the right thing. As a young Christian, I yearned to be more loving than I was. I foolishly prayed, "Lord, help me to feel love." I soon found that I was praying for myself instead of for others. I had my own interests at heart. In addition,

I was viewing love as strictly emotional so that when I prayed for love, I was actually praying for a feeling, an understanding of love I had brought to the Bible from the world. On both counts, praying for myself and praying for a feeling, I was asking *"amiss."*

Study Biblical "Love"

The key to the next principle is found in the epistle to the Philippians, *"And this I pray, that your love may abound yet more and more in knowledge and in all judgment"* (Phil. 1:9). How does love abound? In knowledge. Knowledge is a missing ingredient in most relationships today. From the first stirrings of love through the wedding day and into the marriage itself, very few see the necessity of studying the subject of love. They major on acting from the heart but have not *"obeyed from the heart that form of doctrine"* (Rom. 6:17). Many engaged couples find their head disengaged by their heart and give little thought to the notion that maybe more than premarital feelings are needed to sustain a relationship. Few married Christians ever attempt any course of premarital study, counseling, or preparation about love and marriage. They are *"destroyed for lack of knowledge."* If love abounds through knowledge, then a vital way to grow love is to increase in knowledge about biblical love itself.

It sounds almost laughable to some to think that love is something you study. Americans have been so conditioned to think of love in terms of spontaneous emotions that the notion of learning about love is a turnoff. I heard of a couple who went to a sold-out play. The wife was sitting between her husband and another man. When the house lights went down, the husband heard a loud smacking sound. "What was that noise?" he asked. "That man just kissed me," she replied. The husband jumped to his feet, saying "Let me at him! I'll teach him a thing or two!" "Sit down," said the wife. "You can't teach him a thing!" We can chuckle at this joke, but it is no joking matter when a married person laughs at the idea of learning how to love God's way. This is understandable for inexperienced youth who are still dazed by the power of newly discovered goose bumps but detrimental for a mature married partner serious about improving his relationship.

Live Out Your Love

There are two strategic principles of human behavior that have long held a fascination for behaviorists. This interest is traceable to the fact that these principles can complement each other as easily as they contradict each other.

The first of these is the belief that all behavior springs out of one's attitude: feelings and/or thoughts. The Bible bears this out: *"For out of the abundance of the heart the mouth speaketh"* (Matt. 12:34). In other words, the heart is the source of actions: *"Ye have obeyed from the heart"* (Rom. 6:17). Some would argue from this viewpoint that all actions are traceable to feelings. Therefore, the way to happiness is to squelch the bad feelings such as guilt and promote good feelings such as love. We have seen this accomplished in America as guilt has been systematically removed via our "victim" vocabulary and placed on the doorstep of some offender. "Love" is judged genuine only if there are deep pleasant feelings connected.

At the same time, feelings become the ultimate motivation for action. The media kingpins know that the way to get ratings is to get to the feelings. Entertainment, especially TV, is geared to the feelings. Strong emotions rule the ratings game: fear, greed, lust, anger, guilt, sorrow, and love are the stars. Politicians know that moving hearts is more vote productive than informing heads.

All this is the natural result of an unhealthy preoccupation with feeling-based living. Any truth out of balance can become heresy, and this is getting mighty close.

The second belief is the darling of true behaviorists. They believe a man can be changed by focusing on his actions. Pavlovian conditioning of behavior changes the conduct of the dog. There is some merit in this argument because it is true that actions can move the heart, producing attitudes and emotions: *"Commit thy works* [actions] *unto the Lord, and thy thoughts shall be established"* (Prov. 16:3).

Which is right? Both are right. Which is wrong? Both are wrong. Confused? It is confusing until you bring these extreme views into balance with one another. They can contradict each other or they can complement each other; the key is balance. The balance comes when equal billing is given to each viewpoint. In the thinking of most husbands and wives, the great majority of training, conditioning, and experience have been on the side of emotions ruling behavior rather than behavior ruling emotions. This is evident by the dependence upon feelings in starting the relationship, sustaining it, and even ending it. It is all based on the feelings of the moment. Some of you reading this are coming at your marriage with one goal: restore the romance. Is that wrong? No, unless like me, you *"ask amiss that ye may consume it upon your feelings,"* oops, I mean *"lusts."* The problem with making feelings instead of ministry the goal is that you tend to wait on the feelings before you act.

Rather than waiting on feelings to control one's expressions of love, each person can cultivate his love through the expressions of love.

When I was pastoring, I yearned for more love for my people. I observed my assistant pastor and admired his love for everyone around him. He hugged as freely as he verbalized his love. I thought to myself, "I should try that. Maybe it will give me some of the love that he has." So I went up to my head usher and looked him in the face and said, "Frank, I love you!" He pawed the carpet with his toe, looked for a quick exit, breathed a hasty "I love you too, preacher" and disappeared. That wasn't so bad, so after some time I thought I should go for the hug as well. I walked up to him and gave him a big bear hug while saying, "I love you." He stiffened up, pointed his chin to the ceiling, and through a reddened face squeaked out an "I love you too" before running for the door. But through all this I noticed something interesting: the more I expressed love, the more I felt love. If it is true that feelings are the dividends that God pays on the investment of obedience, then I was enjoying the fruit of my investment. Too many wait for the feelings to control the expression of love, perhaps feeling hypocritical or phony if the feelings aren't there. But if the expression of love is action, *"God so loved . . . that he gave,"* and if action is obedience, then the gift of expressed love will be honored by God in time with true feelings of love.

If you feel love for your mate, show it freely, but don't wait on feelings to show love. To do so is to be the slave of your feelings. You can choose at any time to minister love through your actions.

Have the Right Goal

That brings us to a question. Why do you want your love to grow? Motives are all-important in the loving process. If love is the fruit, motives are the root, for *"out of it* [the heart] *are the issues of life"* (Prov. 4:23).

The best test of our motives is to compare them with God's. God's motive for love is revealed in the Scriptures: *"The Lord make you to increase and abound in love . . . to the end he may stablish your hearts unblameable in holiness"* (I Thess. 3:12–13). Notice that His purpose in the increase of your love is not that you can feel good, not that you can be happy, not even that you can enjoy some relief from your painful circumstances; His purpose is holiness! I often ask my counselees why they have come for counseling. If their answer is "happiness," I reply, "then I can't help you." Why do I say this? Because I know that a prerequisite to progress in counseling is the motive of the counselee. James put it this way: *"Ye ask, and receive not, because ye ask amiss, that ye may consume it upon your lusts"* (James 4:3). The way to avoid asking *"amiss"* is to ask according to God's motive and purpose: your holiness.

How does love produce holiness? Jesus admonished us to *"love . . . thy God . . .* [and] *love thy neighbor as thyself"* (Matt. 22:37, 39) and with good reason. *"On these two commandments hang all the law and the prophets"* (v. 40). A brief look at the Ten Commandments will illustrate this. The first five have to do with our walk with God; the last five have to do with our walk with our neighbor. Love will ensure that these commandments remain unbroken. If I love God, will I have any other gods before Him? No. Will I make a graven image? No. Will I take God's name in vain? No. Will I remember the Sabbath? Yes. Then the degree of my holiness depends upon the degree of my love for God. What about my neighbor? If I love, will I honor my father and mother? Yes. Will I kill? No. If I love my mate, will I commit adultery with another? No. Will I steal, lie, or covet? No! What keeps me from sinning against God and others? My love for them. So then, love produces holiness! God knew that and set holiness before us as the ultimate motive and goal of all love, *"to the end he may stablish your hearts unblameable in holiness."*

Be Committed

You have learned some vital principles of growing your love, but what is to ensure that you persevere in your growth? It is the principle of commitment, being committed for the long haul. *"And let us not be weary in well doing: for in due season we shall reap, if we faint not"* (Gal. 6:9). *"Therefore . . . be ye steadfast, unmoveable, always abounding in the work of the Lord"* (I Cor. 15:58). A common mistake of naive newly marrieds is to fail to consider that time may have a negative effect on their love. The mistake of discouraged marriage veterans is to fail to realize that time can have a positive effect on their love. At the beginning you "fell in love." Now you must "grow in love." What is the difference? At first you seemed to have no control over your love. Now God is given control of your love. And what does He do with it? *"The Lord make you to increase and abound in love."*

"Divorce" is a word that should be cut out of every couple's dictionary. It should never be brought up in a conversation, much less considered. Couples who have found themselves in divorce court didn't land there by chance. They went through a lengthy process of thinking about it, seriously considering it, and even discussing it in moments of tension. If *"evil communications corrupt good manners"* (I Cor. 15:33), then enough talking and thinking about divorce can result in it.

I once officiated at the wedding of a young sailor and his bride in a beautiful ceremony. Some weeks later I observed this couple jokingly refer to one another as "dummy" or "stupid." I warned them that even jokingly they could not talk about the other with those words without experiencing a negative impact upon their marriage. Soon their joking turned more serious and gradually deteriorated into anger that thrust them into heated arguments. They no longer laughed when they called one another "dummy"—now they meant it! I was heartbroken to see them divorce, but I was not greatly surprised. Their evil communications had corrupted something very precious. When people entertain and even express evil thoughts, sinful actions are the result.

Until the back door of divorce is closed, the temptation to run through it will always be there when there is trouble in the house. Instead of oiling the hinges, nail it shut and board it over. Then, when conflicts arise in the marriage, you know there is no easy way out but to work through it. That is commitment.

12

The Missing Element in Communication

A couple had just returned from celebrating their fiftieth wedding anniversary. After a day of festivities they were preparing for bed. As was their custom over the years, he prepared them a nighttime snack of toast and jam with milk. When he placed his wife's portion on the table, she suddenly burst into tears. "What is wrong, honey?" he asked. "I would think that after fifty years of marriage you would give me a piece of the loaf other than the heel!" she sobbed. He replied, "But, honey, the heel is my favorite piece of the loaf." Do you see a breakdown in communication here?

The most common complaint I hear in my marriage counseling is "We just can't seem to communicate!" Sixty percent of divorces in America are sparked by poor communication. What is wrong?

The couple above were both looking at the same thing but in different ways, with divisive perceptions that needed alignment. For any couple to have a heart-to-heart talk, it is necessary to achieve the basic step of aligning these perceptions for a common understanding.

There is no question that there is a need to examine our communication techniques. What comes naturally usually doesn't work. Marriage is a spiritual union; therefore, there is a spiritual communion that defies mere human tools and philosophies. There are scores of books, videos, and other things that promote a worldly approach to communication, but they simply are not suitable for developing intimacy at a spiritual level.

To attempt to have meaningful communication while avoiding the spiritual dimension of the Christian marriage is unthinkable but common nonetheless. Most people who ignore the spiritual element convey an impression to others of which they have little knowledge. In the Gospel of Luke, one of Jesus' disciples lost patience with the Samaritans. Christ had set his face toward Jerusalem in His determination to get there and apparently offended the Samaritans. He had sent some envoys ahead to make arrangements in one of their villages, but because they knew that the Lord had no plans to give His time to them, they would not receive Him. This infuriated two of the disciples, who made a ghastly proposal to Jesus: *"Lord, wilt thou that we command fire to come down from heaven, and consume them, even as Elias did?"* (Luke 9:54). Jesus *"turned, and rebuked them, and said, Ye know not what manner of spirit ye are of"* (Luke 9:55).

Most everybody communicates in this way. We know not the spirit we are conveying. We need to bring that spirit to the Word of God for evaluation. We dare not follow our heart and rely upon our natural instinctive means of communication. We must grow in grace in this most vital of ministries called communication. There is a right way and a wrong way to reach the heart of our loved ones.

How do we do this? We must first start by understanding the crucial elements of communication. What are they?

Facts

Facts are the foundation stones upon which the house of communication rests. They provide the credibility the Bible refers to when we *"speak the truth"* and allow the speaker to *"provide things honest in the sight of all men"* (Rom. 12:17). Without facts there is no honest communication, but with them you can begin to open true and intimate communication lines with your loved one.

Feelings

Feelings are the emotions I experience that are based on my view of the facts. It is possible to speak factually without emotions, but some facts are rife with potential feelings. It is one thing to say, "I had an accident in the car on the way home." It is quite another to say, "I had an accident and killed a pedestrian." Both statements are factual, but one is certainly more loaded with feelings than the other.

Feelings not only vary from circumstance to circumstance but they also vary from personality to personality. Men are often considered to be more factual in their communications than women. Perhaps this is because they spend most of their day in factual communication at work, or maybe it is because they are often more logical in their thinking. The gentler gender, on the other hand, can be more emotional. Their tender spirits and sensitive hearts, which make them wonderful mothers and lovers, may contribute to this generalized distinction.

Men tend to be in touch with their thoughts first and then their feelings while women tend to be in touch with their feelings first and then their thoughts. If you ask a man, "How do you feel?" he may respond by telling you what he's thinking. If you ask a woman "How do you feel?" she will probably tell you what she is feeling. If a man wants to get to his wife's thoughts, he may first have to listen to her feelings. If a woman wants to get to her husband's feelings, she may first have to listen to his thoughts. Of course, this is not to say that a man is incapable of heartfelt feelings any more than it is to say that a woman is incapable of logical reasoning.

Perceptions

Perceptions are the conclusions formed from my view of the facts and the feelings they generate. For example, there are four children standing on the street corner. A dog walks up to them. It is obviously a friendly dog: wagging tail, silly grin, tongue lolling out of one side of his mouth. "Look at the pretty dog!" the children exclaim as they reach out to pet him. But one of the children, a little girl, shrinks back with a look of horror and fear registered on her face. "What's wrong with you!" the other children demand. "It's only a dog!" What they don't know is that the little girl was attacked by a dog just a few months prior, and mauled almost to the point of death.

Watch carefully. Fact: dog is present. Feeling: fear. Perception: danger. The perception of the girl is drastically different from that of her friends. And the result is a great gap in their understanding and communication. She is considered strange because she is not like the others and is therefore shut out from the group. Unless there is a way to bridge the gap between them, there will be no communication. How can the three children reach out to this little girl? The key to this is mercy.

MERCY

"Blessed are the merciful: for they shall obtain mercy" (Matt. 5:7). What is mercy? It is my commitment to appeal to another's perceptions for the purpose of ministering to him at the level of his need. It is crawling inside someone else's skin, feeling what he feels, and on the basis of the understanding gleaned, ministering to him.

Perceptions vary greatly from one person to another. Each person possesses his own set of perceptions that affect his life. Perceptions can vary so drastically from one person to another that I have coined a term that helps me in my counseling: "perceptual reality." This means that each person's reality is grounded in his or her perceptions. That doesn't make it right, and it certainly doesn't alter true reality, but it is where each person lives. If you want to help, you will have to go where he lives. The Scriptures suggest that different people see the same thing in differing ways: *"One man esteemeth one day above another: another esteemeth every day alike. . . . To him that esteemeth any thing to be unclean, to him it is unclean"* (Rom. 14:5–14). A key to communication, then, is to learn where our mate lives, but the tendency is to devote our efforts to getting our mate to come to where we live rather than going to where he or she is. In fact, many marriages deteriorate into a scratching, clawing effort to get the other mate to "understand me." We are naturally more conscious of our own needs and sensitive to them than we are to those of our mate. It requires a spiritual empowerment to unlearn the fleshly response and develop a spiritual one.

It is not difficult to show mercy to the young. We easily spot the needs of little children. I have seen grown men reduced to babbling idiots in the presence of a babe in arms. Why? They are talking baby talk as if the child can understand them. It is cute to watch this because it demonstrates a man's understanding of a child's need. We not only understand this; we practice it.

While I was visiting a pastor's home, their little five-year-old girl interrupted our "adult talk" by walking into the room clutching a doll in each hand. In her right hand she held a Barbie doll and in her left hand she had a Ken doll. Still wearing her Sunday dress, she walked up to me, placed one doll on each of my knees, looked earnestly into my eyes, and asked, "Brudder Binney, will you play dolls with me?" Now, I have always had a soft spot for little girls, and I was melting fast. Her mother was aghast. "Now, honey, don't bother Dr. Binney." But those big eyes had never left mine. Their silent pleading did me in. "I would love to play dolls," I announced to her shocked parents. The girl moved around to the other side of the coffee table and I knelt across from her. She kept the Barbie and handed me the Ken (thankfully). She began bouncing Barbie up and down on the table while talking in a high, squeaky falsetto voice. I bounced Ken up and down and talked back in a basso profundo voice. We had a wonderful conversation.

There seems to be a built-in sensitivity to children and their need of mercy, doesn't there? But let that little child grow into an adult's body, and the automatic assumption is that she doesn't need to be understood any longer. After all, she is an adult just like me and should get a grip. My niece, as a twelve-year-old, was a prematurely tall and statuesque blond, towering over her peers. Her natural beauty and stature gave the impression every child yearns for: maturity. She looked years older than she really was. A problem soon surfaced, however, in the way she was perceived, not by her friends but by adults. They automatically assumed knowledge, ability, and experience beyond her years. As I observed this, I realized that married couples are guilty of the same thing. They look at this big strong man or this mature lovely lady in an adult body and assume that he or she possesses adult perceptions. The truth is that most of us will spend a lifetime strengthening, honing, and improving the perceptions we brought into adulthood from childhood.

Mercy is the missing element in communication of most married couples today. It is the key to building a bridge between the perception of one person and that of another. If the three children had practiced mercy with the little girl who was afraid of the dog, they would have forged bonds of friendship rather than destroying them. If you will learn to apply mercy in your marriage, you will experience a revolution in your intimate communication. To help your understanding, let's think first about . . .

What Mercy Is Not

Feeling Sorry for Someone in Trouble

Mercy is not merely feeling sorry for someone in trouble. We sometimes think that this is the totality of mercy. While it is a very real part, it is often confused as the whole. Mercy is much more.

Uncontrollable Emotions

Mercy is not uncontrollable emotions. The jurors of the infamous Menendez brothers' trial wept as they heard the testimonies of two boys who had murdered their parents. They were weeping over the alleged abuse the boys had suffered at the hands of their father. The media called these tears of mercy. No, mercy is not merely a sickly sentimentality that expresses itself uncontrollably.

OVERLOOKING OF SIN

Mercy is not the overlooking of sin. When truck driver Reginald Denny pled for mercy for his attackers, who had kicked and stoned him almost to death, many applauded his mercy. He justified their behavior based on their environment and upbringing. As commendable as his misguided concern might have been, it was not mercy.

GRACE

Mercy is not grace. Lloyd-Jones explains: "'Grace is especially associated with men in their sins; mercy is especially associated with men in their misery.' In other words, while grace looks down upon sin as a whole, mercy looks especially upon the miserable consequences of sin."[1] W. E. Vine agrees, "Grace describes God's attitude toward the law-breaker and the rebel; mercy is His attitude toward those who are in distress."[2] As grace is directed toward the sinner, mercy is directed toward the sufferer, even when the suffering is a result of sin. It is a ministry toward a person in distress.

A GUARANTEE

Mercy is not a guarantee of your mate's reciprocation of mercy. When Jesus said, *"Blessed are the merciful: for they shall obtain mercy,"* He was not saying, "If you show mercy to others, they will show mercy back to you." Such an interpretation would color our ministries and taint our motives. If the only reason you showed mercy was to get mercy, then it was never a ministry of mercy to begin with. It was an investment. It reveals a spirit wanting help rather than a helpful spirit.

Rather, this verse is saying, "If you show mercy to others, God will show mercy to you." The psalmist writes, *"With the merciful thou wilt show thyself merciful"* (Ps. 18:25).

It is helpful to see what mercy is not because some of you are not gifted with mercy and will find the concept very unappealing especially if you assume it fits in one of the above categories. We must see it from a biblical perspective if we want to make a biblical application.

What Mercy Is

The word "mercy" comes from the Greek word *eleemon* and involves three specific things that are especially meaningful to marital communication. First, it involves conscious and decisive thought; second, it includes a shared pain; and third, it is demonstrated by deliberate action.

Conscious and Decisive Thought

A misleading assumption about love is that it is confined to the emotions. Because of this belief, many assume that expressions of love devoid of feelings cannot be true love. But Jesus taught that you can love with the mind. *"Thou shalt love the Lord thy God with all thy . . . mind"* (Matt. 22:37). One means of loving your mate with the mind is through the ministry of mercy. How is this done?

First, it involves a decision of the mind to truly understand your mate's needs, especially those that require mercy. The husband is admonished to dwell with his wife *"according to knowledge"* (I Pet. 3:7), and the couple is exhorted to submit *"yourselves one to another"* (Eph. 5:21). These admonitions include making a conscious decision to seek to understand the deep needs of your mate.

Second, it involves focusing your thoughts squarely on those needs. This implies a focus and concentration for the purpose of understanding more deeply. When you *"bear one another's burdens,"* you become more conscious of the consequences of those burdens in the life of your mate. When the Lord Jesus saw the needs and burdens of the multitudes, that *"they fainted and were scattered abroad, as sheep having no shepherd,"* His heart was touched. And He *"was moved with compassion on them"* (Matt. 9:36). A basic understanding of your mate's needs is the first step in showing him or her mercy.

Third, mercy will lead you to a decision to go further than just understanding to focusing on your mate's needs. You will be moved to make a decision to *do* something to meet those needs.

This is the first dimension of true biblical mercy. It is a decision that "demands a quite deliberate effort of the mind and the will."[3] Until that effort is made, mercy cannot begin.

In our precounseling questionnaire, we request the counselee to list three things he or she thinks his or her mate would "most like to discuss." It is not unusual to find those blanks empty or with a note attached such as "I don't have a clue." If one mate doesn't know this basic need of the other, the beginning place for them is to make a decision to discover those needs, understand them, focus on them, and minister to them.

This is what Christ did. He thought about His estate of equality with God and made a decision to not hold on to it but rather to become like man; *"Who, being in the form of God, thought it not robbery to be equal with God: but made himself of no reputation, and took upon him the form of a servant, and was made in the likeness of men"* (Phil. 2:6–7). *"It behoved him to be made like unto his brethren."* Why? *"That he might be a merciful and faithful high priest* [unto them]*"* (Heb. 2:17). Christ's ministry of mercy began with a decision.

A Shared Pain

If the first step of ministering mercy is to look at your mate with an eye to finding his need, the next step is to understand that need in a meaningful way. The best way to do that is to enter into it, feel it, share it with your mate. This is sympathy in the literal sense of the word. "Sympathy" is derived from two Greek words, *syn*, which means "together with," and *paschein*, which means "to experience or suffer." Sympathy means "experiencing things together with the other person— literally going through what he is going through."[4] This is an identification with the needs of your mate and a sharing of his or her pain and inward suffering. Mercy "means the ability to get right inside the other person's skin until we can see things with his eyes, think things with his mind, and feel things with his feelings."[5]

A man walking down a city sidewalk past a grade school saw an unusual sight—a circle of children, all of whom were weeping and clutching their stomachs. Upon investigation he noticed that in the center of the circle a boy was lying on the ground, arms wrapped around his midsection, crying loudly. He asked one of the children in the circle, "What is going on here?" She replied, "We're all having a pain in Jimmy's stomach." This is mercy. This is the high calling of every believer when another believer is in distress: *"Whether one member suffer, all the members suffer with it"* (I Cor. 12:26). It is also the basis of compassionate prayer: *"Remember them that are in bonds, as bound with them; and them which suffer adversity, as being yourselves also in the body"* (Heb. 13:3).

We can be thankful that we have in our Lord Jesus Christ an intercessor who can suffer with us. Because He can, He is mercifully motivated to appeal to God for our needs. *"For we have not an high priest which cannot be touched with the feeling of our infirmities; but was in all points tempted like as we are, yet without sin"* (Heb. 4:15). He crawled inside our skin so that He could feel what we feel, and therefore minister to our individual needs. *"For in that he himself hath suffered . . . he is able to succour them that are tempted"* (Heb. 2:18).

Christ made a decision to leave the splendor of heaven to come down to earth in human form. This "incarnation of Christ," as it is known, is seen in His birth as a baby in the manger. He began life as a baby and ended life as an adult; therefore, He knows how the little child feels, He knows how the junior and teenager feel, and He knows how the adult feels. He is touched with the feeling of our infirmities because He shared our pain. On that basis, we are told to take advantage of His mercy when we need His help: *"Let us therefore come boldly unto the throne of grace, that we may obtain mercy, and find grace to help in time of need"* (Heb. 4:16). In like manner, we need to enter into the feelings of our loved ones.

A Deliberate Action

Of course, this understanding and shared pain will never be identical to what your mate is experiencing, but the point is not perfect understanding or feelings but a perfection of effort to understand. It is the effort and only the effort that is seen by your mate. He cannot measure your feelings, gauge your sympathy, or rate your understanding. But he can see your efforts and experience your ministry to him. Lloyd-Jones describes mercy as "a sense of pity plus a desire to relieve the suffering . . . inward sympathy and outward acts in relation to the sorrows and sufferings of others."[6] It is these "outward acts" that are the ultimate measure of true mercy; and when combined with thought and feelings, they lend power to mercy in the marriage relationship.

When the love of God is described in the Bible, it is not in terms of feelings but of action. *"God so loved the world, that he* gave" (John 3:16). If you want to understand the love of Christ, it is His actions you are told to note: *"Hereby perceive we the love of God, because he laid down his life for us"* (I John 3:16). The ultimate expression of mercy is found not so much in what we feel but in what we do.

CONCLUSION

Sandra and I once hosted a getaway for pastors' wives at the manor. We had long been burdened that they have special needs, and we desired to minister to them. Over a period of several days we fed them, counseled them, and in general, tried to make them feel special and loved. As we gathered around the fireplace for prayer one evening, I asked if they had any needs for which we could pray. One wife who was staring into the fire said quietly, "I've never told anyone this before," and proceeded to tell of a painful sexual molestation as a child. As she wept, the other ladies gathered around to hug her as we prayed for her.

Afterwards we asked her, "If you've never told anyone before, why did you choose this place and this time to let it be known?" I will never forget her response. With tears in her eyes, she replied, "Because I felt this was a safe place."

Everyone needs a safe place. You need it and your mate needs it. Does your marriage partner see your arms as a safe place? Your heart?

When he does, and he senses your mercy, he will have found the missing element of communication.

---

[1] D. Martyn Lloyd-Jones, *Studies in the Sermon on the Mount* (Grand Rapids: Wm. B. Eerdmans Publishing Co., 1971), 99.

[2] W. E. Vine, *An Expository Dictionary of New Testament Words* (Westwood, N.J.: Fleming H. Revell Co., 1940), 61.

[3] William Barclay, *The Gospel of Matthew*, vol. 1 (Philadelphia: The Westminster Press, n.d.), .

[4] Barclay.

[5] Barclay.

[6] Lloyd-Jones.

13

A Journey of Discovery: How God Taught Me the Value of Mercy

While I was pastoring a church, Sandra and I would go through a regular ritual on the trip home after the Sunday evening service. I would ask her, "How did you like my sermons today?" Of course, what I meant to say but could not under machismo restraints was "Tell me how wonderful I am!" or "Tell me that Charles Haddon Spurgeon would genuflect in my presence after such a homiletical masterpiece!" But, of course, I couldn't grovel like that. To do so would have been beneath my dignity as a preacher. So I gave her the opportunity to really tell me on her own how great I was. A summary usually went something like this: "Too long, too loud, too deep, and I didn't understand the joke you told, but other than that it was all right." Now, a nominally intelligent person would learn that after a time or two of this, it is best to either change the line of questioning or drop it altogether. But I have never pled guilty to being intelligent, so I repeated this scenario every week for several years. In defense of my wife, I kept her in the dark about my real motivation in asking for her opinion. What she didn't know was that I was appealing to her on the basis of my perception of feeling unworthy or insecure as a preacher and that I needed some support. If I had told her that up front, she would have reassured me. As it was though, she answered me according to her perceptions.

Sandra is a secure, self-assured woman who is my strong right arm in our ministry. Because of her strength and stability, she has never needed a lot of compliments. Actually, she prefers a good honest critique of her needs and shortcomings so that she can shore them up. To her, then, expressions of love are those that help to improve what is not already perfect. When she critiqued me so honestly, it was her way of loving me. I, on the other hand, would rarely critique her appearance, her performance, and so forth because I would not want to hurt her.

I recall one occasion when a nationally recognized pastor and his wife hosted us at their church in a comfortable missionary house. We were invited out for a special night of fellowship and were taken to one elegant restaurant for the main course and another for dessert. In the interim, we were given the red carpet treatment in seeing the sights of the town. At the end of this wonderful evening, we returned to the missionary house to retire. I kicked my shoes off, threw my suit coat over the back of the couch, and plopped down to relax. A moment later I heard a shriek coming from the bedroom. This was not a "mouse-sighting" shriek, not a "cockroach-sighting" pitch. This was not even a personal injury sound. It was different from anything I had ever heard! I jumped to my feet and ran into the bedroom. There was Sandra, staring into the mirror with an expression of shocked disbelief. "Why didn't you tell me?" she demanded. On her left ear she was wearing a white earring, and on the right ear she had a black one. I lamely replied, "Honey, I was always on one side of you or the other." "Yes," she said, "but the other couple was always across from me." If the truth were known, however, I probably would have hesitated to tell her for fear of spoiling her evening.

Just as I never told Sandra my real motivation in asking her opinion of my preaching, she never told me her motivation for answering so honestly. We both were communicating in a way we preferred others to communicate with us.

It would have helped greatly if the Lord had shown us some means of better understanding how to reach the other at our own level of perception. Thankfully, He did. Over time He brought several insights to our attention that turned this around and set us on solid footing.

MINISTERING TO YOUR MATE'S SPIRITUAL GIFT

The first thing we learned, almost by accident, was that we possessed decidedly different and distinct spiritual gifts. I had attended a seminar on spiritual gifts, and I was struck with these differences. When I returned home, I showed Sandra a list of the characteristics of what I thought to be her particular spiritual gift. I did not tell her what she was reading. "That's me!" she exclaimed. "That's me too! What is this stuff? Where did you get it?" she wanted to know. We learned that she had the gift of prophecy and I had the gift of mercy. I also learned that a person with the gift of prophecy has a particular style of communicating to others and desires a direct approach. She, on the other hand, studied my gift of mercy and adapted her style of communication to my needs. What a difference!

We learned to value these differences in one another and to tailor our communication to accommodate them. This was the beginning of a new understanding between us.

MINISTERING TO YOUR MATE'S TEMPERAMENT

Shortly after this, we discovered that we had our own unique blend of temperaments that further colored our communications. "Temperament is the combination of inborn traits that subconsciously affects man's behavior."[1] It is "the characteristic . . . of an individual's nature . . . dependent on constitutional make-up, and . . . largely hereditary in origin."[2] In other words, temperament is a part of your personality that sets you apart as an individual and affects the way you view life and how you respond to the people around you, especially your mate.

Like spiritual gifts, temperaments are a means of measuring the perceptions of the person to whom you are talking. The basic difference in spiritual gifts and temperaments is that gifts are taught in the Scriptures and temperaments are not. That is not to say that temperaments are unbiblical, only nonbiblical. The fact that something is nonbiblical is not necessarily an indictment against it.

DANGERS IN STUDYING TEMPERAMENTS

Some counselors have come out strongly against temperaments as ungodly and anti-Bible. I believe that they are addressing the extremes of interpretation and the abuses inherent in the teaching of temperaments rather than in their intrinsic worth.

Temperaments are not scientific. Their strength lies in their help in determining the perceptions of your mate, and perceptions are too subjective to be scientifically quantified. They can change due to time, seasons of life, and unique circumstances (especially stress). But overall, there is a consistent pattern that emerges. If not careful, a person can misuse temperaments as a synthetic form of sanctification. By attempting to strengthen the weaknesses and to exploit the strengths inherent in the different personality styles, he may adopt a fleshly substitute for spiritual growth.

Other dangers include the justification of sin with a flippant, "Well, that's just my temperament. I can't help being that way. You just have to learn to put up with me." If someone doesn't use these excuses to justify his own sins, they may be used to justify another's sins.

Fatalism is a threat in the study of temperaments, as is justification of sin. Fatalism says that your fate is sealed and your circumstances are permanently fixed; your personality therefore can never be altered. Upon discovering your temperament, there is a temptation to hunker down into a mindset of unchanging permanency while singing "I Shall Not Be Moved."

RIGHT MOTIVES NEEDED

There are right reasons and wrong reasons to study temperaments. The right reason for studying them would be to better understand your mate, to increase your understanding of his or her unique perceptions, and to find help in better ministering mercy.

The wrong reasons would be to understand yourself, to get your mate to understand you, to try to predict the responses of others, or to use this knowledge as a power leverage in controlling or manipulating your mate.

At the Moorehead Manor, I give a profile to help identify both the counselee's spiritual gift and his temperament. I find these to be invaluable in counseling. It gives me a visible measurement of a person's self-perception that aids me greatly. I now have a tool by which to understand the unique perceptions of an individual that removes much of the guesswork in my counseling.

It also removes the guesswork in communications for the marriage partners. For many couples, it represents the first time that one mate now can see why and how perceptions of the other mate differ so drastically in their communication.

Sandra's basic temperament is choleric. The greatest fear of a choleric is to be taken advantage of; she likes to be approached directly, and she has an ability to see the big picture and to discern what is lacking in a project. Understanding this about her has helped me to appeal to her perceptions.

My basic temperament is phlegmatic. A phlegmatic's greatest fear is conflict and loss of security. His strength is an unflappable steadfastness under fire. As a corpsman in the navy, my temperament was tailor-made for my role in the emergency room. It made little difference if I were handed amputated limbs or a lifeless baby. I would maintain a calmness that at the time amazed even me.

CONCLUSION

And so began a journey that continues to this day, a journey of discovery about how to minister mercy to one another. Frustration can give way to blessing when you set out to communicate to your mate's unique perceptions by the merciful acts of communication. It made a difference for us; it can for you as well.

---

[1] Tim LaHaye, *Spirit-Controlled Temperament* (Wheaton, Ill.: Tyndale House Publishers, 1966), 5.

[2] Gordon Allport quoted in *Baker Encyclopedia of Psychology and Counseling*, ed. David Benner and Peter C. Hill (Grand Rapids: Baker Books, 1999), 1200.

14

TAKING AIM: ESTABLISHING GOALS IN THE MINISTRY OF COMMUNICATION

I once read that only 5 percent of Americans set goals for their lives, and yet of those who do, 95 percent reach them. I wonder how many married couples set any goals for their marriage, and specifically for their communication. This chapter is about the goals you need to have in mind as you set out to talk heart to heart with your mate.

THE DIFFERENCE BETWEEN A "GOAL" AND A "DESIRE"

Anytime you think about setting goals, it is vital to keep them separate from your desires, to know the distinction between the two. What is the difference?

A goal is an objective under my direct control; if it is not under my control, I am foolish to assume responsibility for it. It is one thing to have a goal of mowing my lawn, it is another to have a goal of mowing Yosemite National Park. Mowing my lawn is something I have the power and ability to accomplish; mowing Yosemite is not. Secondly, a goal is something that I and I alone am responsible for attaining. I have a keen sense of personal responsibility for achieving this. Thirdly, my response to a goal is action. I do it.

A desire is different from a goal. It is something I would like to accomplish but realize that I do not have the power or the control to achieve. Only God has. Therefore, I must not take any responsibility upon myself for reaching it. The proper response to a desire is prayer.

It should never be a goal to change another person. It can be a desire for which you pray but it must not be a goal. Why is this? Because a human being's mind, heart, and will are involved, and that is God's exclusive domain and not to be presumed upon.

Let us be reminded of the effectual power of God in working in the human life. He changes the thinking or beliefs of man: *"And you that were sometime alienated and enemies in your mind by wicked works . . . now hath he reconciled"* (Col. 1:21). Who was it that turned your wicked mind from sin to the Savior? It was God: *"No man can come to me, except the Father . . . draw him"* (John 6:44). As God has worked in your life, He can do the same for your mate. If you think you can change the thinking of your mate, you will experience frustration if you fail, or experience pride if you succeed; but in neither case, will you have relied upon God to do the changing.

God is also in control of the human heart: *"The king's heart is in the hand of the Lord, as the rivers of water: he turneth it whithersoever he will"* (Prov. 21:1). The rivers in question are not those like the mighty Mississippi or Ohio; it is a reference to the irrigation ditches on a farmer's land. A hand-operated gate determines whether the flow of water will run to the back forty acres or the front forty. The farmer puts his hand on a lever, and at his whim, changes the direction of the water. In like manner, God has His hand squarely upon the lever that controls the direction of the king's heart. The emphasis here is on the king because in the time of the writing of Proverbs, an earthly king was the most independently powerful person known to man.

The Bible records that when Saul was anointed king, *"God gave him another heart"* (I Sam. 10:9), and He gave Solomon a *"wise and understanding heart"* (I Kings 3:12), in both cases to equip them to serve Him as king.

The changing of the human heart, then, is the exclusive prerogative of God. Even the apostle Paul gave God all the credit for the change in the lives of the Roman Christians: *"God be thanked, that ye were the servants of sin, but ye have obeyed from the heart"* (Rom. 6:17).

God even orchestrates the will of man for His purposes: *"For it is God which worketh in you both to will and to do of his good pleasure"* (Phil. 2:13). God's people are made willing by the power of God: *"Thy people shall be willing in the day of thy power"* (Ps. 110:3). The will of your mate is under the rulership of God.

You are not capable of changing your mate; therefore, you are certainly not responsible to do so. Since only God can, your response to the need of change is to appeal to God, who is able to change the mind, the heart, and the will.

As a young Christian, I was encouraged to have a goal of winning a certain number of souls to Christ each week. I was also told that in order to reach this goal, several things were needful. First, don't waste time; if someone has not responded within a few minutes, I should leave him and witness to another lost soul who has more interest and a better chance of being saved. Second, control the conversation to insure that the gospel was presented in a fluid and expeditious manner. Put off any questions until the person has prayed to be saved. Third, ask questions that could elicit only a "yes" response. The more often a person said "yes," the more likely he would be to say "yes" to the invitation to pray. "You believe the Bible don't you?" "You want to go to heaven when you die, right?" "Wouldn't you like to bow your head right now and trust Christ as your Savior?" (While I was asking these questions, I was also nodding my head in the affirmative to further insure a positive response. I actually saw people bow their head to pray while nodding with me.) Fourth, lead him in a word-by-word prayer to insure that he did not make a mistake in his prayer for salvation. Fifth, be sure to convince him that what he just did guaranteed his salvation for all time. Then I would write his name in my New Testament as another victory and leave.

Now, it doesn't take a lot of imagination to realize that this was a spiritual form of high pressure. The goal was to get a name on the dotted line. It smacked of a salesmanship technique more suited to a door-to-door salesman than to a representative of God. I must confess, however, that it worked! It worked, that is, if your definition of success was a certain number of "converts," because there were many. The woods out there are full of my converts even today, though I'm not so sure that they are God's converts. That's because I had pressured them into a decision. Pressuring another for a response is the natural consequence of viewing his change as a goal.

At some point, I became uneasy with this approach. I experienced conviction from God that I was orchestrating this scenario apart from His role. I became conscious that it had to be God who saves a soul and changes a life. My goal gradually changed from that of seeing a definite number of souls saved per week to seeking witnessing opportunities. I no longer had a goal of getting men and women to pray the sinner's prayer but of clearly and thoroughly presenting the gospel. I exchanged the goal of putting off their questions for the goal of thoroughly answering their questions so they could come to God with their whole heart. I even inserted two new questions into my presentation: "Is there any reason why you would not want to trust Christ today?" And "As you have heard all this from the Bible, do you have a desire to be saved?" The result? Fewer decisions but a higher percentage of public professions and of faithfulness to Christ. The difference? It was not up to me to pressure people into heaven. I now saw the winning of a soul as a desire, and I changed my focus from arm-twisting manipulation to knee-bending intercession. My trust was no longer in my ability but God's. My goal had become a desire.

Now the goal was within my power and my responsibility so I acted on it. By making the goal that of clearly presenting the gospel, I could always reach it. By making it a desire to see them saved, I found myself praying more and more.

Here then are the clear dangers of confusing a desire with a goal when it comes to changing another person. You resort to manipulation, take credit for success, feel guilty for failure, and also utilize coercion to remake this person into the image you have for him. A more subtle consequence is that you deflect the responsibility for all change upon your mate, especially if you see change as the primary issue. And let's not forget the issue of God's glory in all this; if you take the credit, He gets none.

When you think of your mate, do you feel it's up to you to change his thinking, his feelings, or his actions toward you? Do you find yourself putting him under pressure to conform to your expectations? Are you driven to intimidate, to punish, to get him to understand your needs? If so, you are probably confusing a goal and a desire.

The words you speak possess an awesome power to heal or to destroy. James tells us, *"The tongue is a fire, a world of iniquity . . . it defileth the whole body, and setteth on fire the course of nature; and it is set on fire of hell. . . . It is an unruly evil, full of deadly poison. Therewith bless we God . . . and . . . curse we men"* (James 3:6–9).

The tongue can be a great means for good: *"Let no corrupt communication proceed out of your mouth, but that which is good to the use of edifying, that it may minister grace unto the hearers"* (Eph. 4:29). That brings us to the first of several goals you must have in communicating with your mate.

Never Corrupt Another

You hold in your hand, or more accurately, in your mouth, the power to hurt your spouse. Like a youth with a new gun, everyone needs to learn the negative power of the tongue before using it. *"Death and life are in the power of the tongue"* (Prov. 18:21). What death can the tongue produce? The Book of Proverbs tells us it can be a burning fire (16:27), separate friends (16:28), expose secrets (20:19), cause deep emotional wounds (26:22), work ruin (26:28), encourage immorality (7:21), and destroy a neighbor (11:9). No wonder the Bible says the tongue has the power of death.

God says that each of us is responsible to insure that these things never happen to another because of our speech. The word *"let"* in *"Let no corrupt communication proceed out of your mouth"* means that you have a choice. You can have a goal to never hurt your partner with your tongue, a goal that is within your reach.

EDIFY YOUR PARTNER

God not only wants your goal to be noncorrupting but also to be edifying. The word "edify" means to build up. "Edifice" is a word used to refer to a building that has been built up, stone upon stone, into an impressive structure. A goal of every married partner should be to always use the kind of language that strengthens and builds up his mate. Like the stones in a building, your words can create a spiritual edifice.

Notice in Proverbs the qualities of godly speech: *"a tree of life"* (15:4), *"bringeth forth wisdom"* (10:31), *"disperse knowledge"* (15:7), and *"feed many"* (10:21). We are told how loving words can encourage another: *"Pleasant words are as an honeycomb, sweet to the soul, and health to the bones"* (16:24); *"heaviness in the heart of man maketh it stoop: but a good word maketh it glad"* (12:25); *"the tongue of the wise is health"* (12:18). Oh, the power of the tongue for good! What a ministry you can have in your marriage! You can build up your mate in so many ways with the words you speak.

MINISTER GRACE TO THE HEARER

A pastor friend told me of his association with the late Roy Hession, well-known revivalist and author. He would regularly greet my friend with the words "Brother, let me pollinate you for a bit," and would then share some blessing of God with him. That's a good picture of ministering grace; as the bee moves about the blossom, the pollen from the plant clings to the tiny hairs on its legs. As it flies from plant to plant, the pollen is transferred from one plant to another. The bee benefits every plant it visits. We should go from heart to heart pollinating others with the blessings of the Word of God. That would make everyone a minister of grace, wouldn't it?

I recall a needy time of my life when I was pollinated by a friend in a big way. I recorded the incident in a booklet written some time ago:

> It was the lowest point of my sixteen years in the pastorate and my entire Christian experience. I was sitting alone in my study with my face in my hands while the tears flowed unhindered down my cheeks. A book that I had been studying sat before me, opened to the story of a preacher who had changed his identity and fled his church and family to escape the pressures of the pastorate. In my despair, I intended to follow the same course. I had never felt so terribly alone. I seemed to be sliding into a black hole of immeasurable despondency, a swirling vortex that gripped me in an inescapable stranglehold. "Oh God," I sobbed, "if you are there, if you can hear me, I have never in my life needed to hear your voice like I do this moment! Please let me know that you care, that you love me!
>
> I had no sooner uttered those words than the telephone began ringing. I don't mind telling you that at that point, I didn't want to answer it. I had never received a phone call from heaven and wasn't sure that I would recognize the voice of God. But after getting my composure, I picked up the receiver; "Hello, Pastor Binney! This is Roger Lemmen, your favorite deacon! I have no idea why I'm calling you, but I was just now in prayer and got the strongest urge to call and tell you that I love you and God loves you. See you on Sunday." Click, the phone went dead.
>
> As I stared dumbly at the receiver in my hand, it slowly dawned on me that God had heard my prayer. I realized that I had just heard from heaven! Words cannot express the waves of joy and peace that swept over my tormented spirit. How blessed I was to have a godly deacon, faithful to minister to his pastor in his hour of need."[1]

Had it not been for that call, that thoughtful word of grace, my life might have been drastically changed. Do you know someone who needs a call? Does your marriage partner need a word of grace from you? It could change his or her life.

A pastor recently called me to let me know that a discouraged couple from his church had come to hear me preach and what they heard had changed their lives. They returned home to become some of his best supporters and the church's hardest workers. "God really used you to do a work of grace in their hearts," the pastor informed me.

Can God use human words to accomplish a work of divine grace? Yes, He can, and He wants to use you to do that same work in everyone who hears you, especially your mate. The choice seems rather clear, doesn't it? You can minister grace or you can minister disgrace.

Speak the Truth in Love

As an unsaved teenage runaway, I was lonely and confused. Hoping to bring some order into my life, I found a large and ornate neighborhood church and slipped into the back pew during a revival service. The speaker was a hell-fire-and-brimstone preacher. "If you are here today without Christ" (was he looking at me?) "and you don't ask Jesus to save you" (he was looking at me!) "when you die" (now he was pointing at me!) "you're gonna go to hell and burn forEVAH!" After this explosion of sound and fury, there was an eerie quiet as he glared at me through bulging eyes and reddened face. I left that day with the gnawing impression that he would have been disappointed had I not gone there. Looking back on that occasion, I am convinced, however, that he spoke the truth.

I decided to try again. I chose a less auspicious place this time, opting for a small storefront building with just a handful of people. Maybe, I figured, the intimacy of the setting would dissuade any hell-fire preaching. I figured wrong. In fact, the preacher said almost the precise words uttered by the previous sinner skinner. "If you are here today without Christ and don't ask Jesus to save you, when you die, you're gonna go to hell and burn forever." The words were similar but the preacher was drastically different from his forerunner. His voice was soft and low, tears welled up in his eyes, and his lips trembled with compassion as he spoke. Same message, same words, different spirit. They both spoke the truth, but this man spoke it in love. I left wanting to give some thought to what this preacher had said because I felt the love behind it.

It is not enough merely to speak the truth. Some misguided souls pride themselves on holding nothing back. What is needed is truth balanced with love. That's a combination that is difficult to resist. How does one speak the truth in love?

Look for the Good

The first thing is to look honestly for some good quality in your mate. By truthfully acknowledging or bragging on that quality, you can encourage your spouse through your words. *"A word fitly spoken is like apples of gold in pictures of silver"* (Prov. 25:11). I have enjoyed seeing many people respond to loving words over the years. It's much like watching a time-lapse video of a flower opening its petals to the rays of the sun. When warm words fall on cold hearts, the effect is dramatic.

I was in east Chicago on a soulwinning visit and came to a small weather-beaten house on a dirty side street. The door was answered by a bedraggled woman and a beggarly child, who was clutching the folds of her mother's dress and peeking shyly at this stranger who had come to visit. "Oh, don't mind her," said the mother, "she's just bashful around strangers."

I was reminded of the saying from east Tennessee: "Give a dawg a bad name, and he'll kill hisself livin' up to it." Mountain people wisely note that people naturally live out the expectations that others have of them. This mother had just given her daughter a bad name, a command of sorts to behave like a bashful person.

"Oh, I don't think she's bashful," I replied. "In fact, I think that we are going to be the best of friends very soon." In less than fifteen minutes, the little girl had crawled up onto my lap and we were playing patty cake fast and furious. The disbelieving mother exclaimed, "I just can't believe it. She's never acted that way with a stranger before." I wanted to reply (but held my tongue), "Maybe it's because nobody ever believed that she could and told her so."

I am absolutely convinced that behind the layers of grime and soot on every human soul, there beats a heart that hungers for that *"word fitly spoken."* Underneath bashful veneers live lonely souls who would love for someone to befriend them and invite them onto their laps.

You can choose to look on the filth and think the worst, or you can think on *"whatsoever things are true . . . honest . . . just . . . pure . . . lovely . . . of good report"* (Phil. 4:8) about the person. When you *"think on these things,"* the result is *"virtue"* and *"praise."* Such words never have more power than when they come from the lips of those closest to you. What a ministry you can have when you speak the truth in love!

Far better that you have this ministry than someone else. Consider the "love bank" concept of human nature. Into this bank go deposits that are compliments, words of praise, and sincere esteem. Out of this bank withdrawals are made as well: criticisms, putdowns, and complaints. When boy meets girl, it is all deposits. Words of love, expressions of admiration and compliments abound. Then comes marriage. After a while the deposits stop. A while longer and the withdrawals start. The love bank gets emptied after enough withdrawals are made. Enter Vivacious Vivian, the vocal vixen, at the husband's office. "My, your wife is lucky to have a husband like you," she coos. Major deposit! And a dangerous one because the ol' empty love bank hasn't seen something like this in a long time. "You seem to be so wise, and I need some help. Could we have lunch together today?" as she wipes a tear from her eye. Another major deposit. After enough of these deposits, and no withdrawals, the empty-hearted, empty-headed man goes like a lamb to the slaughter. *"For the lips of a strange woman drop as a honeycomb, and her mouth is smoother than oil: but her end is bitter as wormwood, sharp as a twoedged sword"* (Prov. 5:3–4).

Your mate may be vulnerable as well if she has an empty love bank. Why not make some deposits?

Frequent Praise

Another way to speak the truth in love is to learn how to praise and compliment your loved one. It's not enough to merely see the good; a mate needs to hear your appreciation of it. I learned that four compliments are required to offset one criticism and maintain a balance of self-worth in a person. Whether that is true or not, anybody is going to respond much more positively to compliments than criticism. A merciful person attracts friends like a blossom draws bees. There is a natural fragrance about such a life. You can have that fragrance by learning to esteem your mate.

As a grandfather, it is a joy to watch the eyes of my grandchildren light up when I brag on them. Recently our granddaughter Mikayla wore a new dress. When she walked into the room, I exclaimed, "Will you look at this little girl! Such a little lady! Has anyone ever seen a little girl who looked more like a princess than her?" I would not trade her smile for anything in the world. She proudly wore her dress to Sunday school and then resisted all efforts to get her to remove it afterwards.

What little children love, older children enjoy also. I recall being called to pastor a church and school for which my wife and I were little prepared. On our first day to the church and school campus, we were greeted by a group of senior high girls in short shorts doing toe touchers with their backs to us. We also found the other girls wearing tight slacks, sporting hard rock T-shirts, and proudly exposing their navels for all to see. My first inclination was to roar into the first chapel session and let these junior-sized Jezebels have it with both barrels! But God led me to take a better approach. I preached on the subject "Girls, You're a Treasure" from the verse in Proverbs *"Who can find a virtuous woman? For her price is far above rubies"* (31:10). I explained the great value of virtue in a girl's life and told them if they wanted a prince, they would have to carry themselves like a princess. I encouraged them to attract boys the Bible way—with a godly countenance and holy life. I concluded by telling them that I believed in my heart that they were ladies and princesses already. They merely needed to dress and act like it. I had no idea how this would be received, but when chapel was over, fifteen girls lined up to thank me for helping them feel like a lady and they expressed their desire to live up to my expectation. When I would see one of them wearing a dress in the school hallway, I would stop to compliment them. In the chapel for the elementary students, I would even seek out the girls with the most frilly dresses and bring them onto the platform to brag on these "little ladies." It was cute to be encountered by other little girls wanting me to see their new dresses.

In time a gradual change took place in the student body. The tight slacks and bare midriffs soon gave way to lovely, feminine skirts and blouses, and all without a rebellious note being heard. What had happened? Words of praise won the day! They always do.

The "Sandwich Approach"

Perhaps one of the best ways to speak the truth in love is to use the "sandwich approach." When painful truth must be given, deliver it like a piece of sandwich meat between two slices of praise and esteem. The effect is to temper any criticism with the buffering layers of love.

While a student in college, I enrolled in a speech class taught by Mrs. Neal. She was a great teacher and much loved by her students. I soon learned why. I was called upon to make the dreaded trip to the front of the class to deliver my first speech. I was petrified. After completing my speech, I just knew that the flag outside the Orators' Hall of Fame had been lowered to half-mast, that the angels had covered their ears with their wings, and I had begun plans for my funeral. But Mrs. Neal, who had watched and listened with great interest, asked me to remain on the platform for the inevitable "critique." "Jim," she began, "that was a very good speech. You had good eye contact and it is obvious that you did some thorough research in preparation for it." Wow! This is great! I am ready to cancel my funeral after all. And then she uttered a three letter word for which speech teachers are famous: "But." "But," she continued, "your third point was weak and you need more inflection in your voice." Reschedule the funeral. "However" (the poor funeral director is getting confused), "I believe that God has gifted you as a speaker and is going to use you greatly for His glory. Keep up the good work. You may step down now." Step down? I floated down to my seat in a daze of conflicting signals, but the overriding conclusion I took with me was that Mrs. Neal liked my speech. More importantly, she liked me! I love the memory of that teacher to this day. She knew how to speak the truth in love to an insecure young man and give him the courage to pursue his vision of Christian service.

The next time you go to critique your mate, why not try the sandwich approach? Preface any complaint with a praise and follow it with a compliment. See if it doesn't make a difference. You say, "But won't my mate catch on after a few times of that?" His mind may sense some flattery, but his hungry spirit won't care. Besides, as my high school football coach was fond of saying, "If you gotta fall, fall forward and get an extra yard!" If you must make a mistake, make it on the side of love. You can be forgiven for loving too much before you will be forgiven for loving too little.

CONCLUSION

As you commit yourself to minister mercy to your marriage partner, keep your goals clearly in mind. You may feel you're aiming at the moon, but at least you've established the target and you're making an effort. Remember that 95 percent of those who establish goals reach them! May God help you to reach yours.

---

[1] Jim Binney, *Holding Up Holy Hands* (New Concord, Ohio: The Counselor's Pen, 1997), 1.

15

Mercy in Action

I am fascinated by a unique idea successfully used in evangelism called the Love Thy Neighbor Banquet. It is based on the concept of loving people to Christ through an active ministry to them. Here's how it works: each church member is asked to target one neighbor; then he is to have a six-month ministry of active love to him. Asking nothing in return, he loves his neighbor by manifesting the love of Christ to him; he takes fresh-baked cookies, mows his lawn, helps with home maintenance, shovels snow from his driveway, washes his car, or does anything else that shows unconditional love. At the end of the six months, he invites his neighbor to go to his church's neighbor-recognition banquet as his special guest of honor. At the banquet the speaker brings a message on "The Good Samaritan" or some other theme that shows the love of God. The speaker explains how Christ can change a man and wants to save each guest present. He then explains that "the person who brought you here tonight has experienced this change." At a signal, every host turns to his neighbor and explains how Christ saved his soul and urges his lost neighbor to consider placing his trust in Christ also. Of course by this time, the neighbor has seen the love of Christ pouring through his Christian neighbor for six full months. He knows it is genuine, and God has fertile soil in which to plant the seed. After the testimonies, the speaker gives a public invitation to call on Christ. Guess who the counselors are? That's right, the neighbors themselves—who better than the person who has been loving that unsaved neighbor all these months? Many people have come to Christ because of this plan that builds a ministry around loving with actions.

Benefits of Actions

A Means of Measuring Real Love

I believe that the reason for the effectiveness of the banquet is that there is an innate desire in every human heart to see the reality of God's love. So much is said about love these days that it has lost its meaning. Love is action. Everyone in every nation understands a hug, a smile, or a gift of food or clothes. God knew it was necessary to prove His love toward us and gave us clear evidence of it. *"Hereby perceive we the love of God, because he laid down his life for us,"* so He let us see the proof of His love. He also expects us to reach out to others in the same way that He reached out to us: *"and we ought to lay down our lives for the brethren"* (I John 3:16). Why should you reach out so dramatically to others? So that they can perceive the love of God through your sacrifice. James says that faith without works is dead. Dead faith never attracted anything but flies, but living works will arrest the attention of the world.

Your mate can always measure your love by your actions. She may not see your feelings, understand your words, or even believe them; but there is no disputing the love behind actions. This was how the early Christians could comprehend God's love, and the love of the brethren as well. It is the way that lost people understand the love of the Christian. It is also the way that your mate will understand your love. Actions of love drown out the words of love every time. *"My little children, let us not love in word, neither in tongue; but in deed and in truth"* (I John 3:18).

Not Dependent on Feelings

If you condition all your expressions of love on your feelings, you can get in line with the vast majority of the rest of the world. But you can also trade in your Christianity for a membership card in the "I-Gotta-Feel-It-First" club. Basing your portrayal of your love solely on how you feel at the moment means that you are the victim of your heart. It rules your actions; you don't. As we have already seen, the heart is the weakest, most defenseless part of man. The circumstances can influence it, your blood sugar can influence it, the mood of the moment can influence it, the response of your mate can influence it, and most important, Satan can influence it.

Why wait on your heart then, when you can show your love at will through your actions? You have the power to override your feelings and show your love whenever your mate needs it, instead of when you need to show it. You control the timing and the means of demonstrating love. If mercy is for the benefit of the other person, the active demonstration of your love benefits them greatly.

You don't determine your expressions of love to your children by your need, but theirs. When your little boy has a "boo-boo," you don't wait until it's convenient or you are emotionally stirred enough to pick him up and kiss him, do you? You might already have a child on one hip, the phone cradled in your shoulder, and supper on the stove, but you take the time because you know he needs it. You may be on a stepladder with a hammer in your hand and a mouthful of nails, but when your child falls from a sawhorse, you don't wait until it is more convenient; you show your love. Your mate needs the same demonstration of love that your child does, and that demonstration is seen through what you do!

Shows a Sacrificial Spirit

How much did God love the world? He *"so loved"* it. How do we know that? He *"gave"*; that's an action. How did Christ show His love for the church? He gave Himself for it. How do you show love for your mate? You give of yourself. You give when it's costly, inconvenient, and serves no selfish purpose. That is love. When you love like that, you demonstrate the sacrificial love of the Father and of the Son.

Promotes More Love

It is axiomatic that grace begets grace; the more you express love, the more you will experience it in your heart. *"Commit thy works unto the Lord, and thy thoughts shall be established"* (Prov. 16:3). If you want to love your mate more fervently, then learn to give of yourself more frequently. The more you show your love, the more your love will grow.

Fulfills God's Means of Ministry

God has a twofold plan for ministering to your mate. He has a *direct route* and He has an *indirect route.*

The direct route is straight from His heart to your mate's heart: *"The love of God is shed abroad in our hearts by the Holy Ghost which is given unto us"* (Rom. 5:5).

The breadth of God's love is revealed in the fact that He is not satisfied in loving us in this way only. He has devised another way to insure that His love finds its way into the life of your partner. He sends it THROUGH YOU. This is the indirect route. He convicts you, saves you, fills you with His Spirit, and then commands you to love your mate. God loves through you to your mate. Think of it. What a joy to be used like this by God! And how does He show His love through you? Through your acts of love and mercy to your spouse.

We have shown you in chapter 12 that mercy is made up of three components: decisive thought, shared pain, and deliberate action. Mercy is not mercy until it is manifested in a spiritually motivated action for the benefit of another. How can the mercy in your heart be shared with your marriage partner through action? What actions are we talking about?

Take the Initiative

Ministry, whenever it is discussed in the Scriptures, is almost always proactive rather than reactive. Even in the face of fierce opposition and in the presence of personal suffering, you demonstrate ministry by acting on the behalf of another. You are to love your enemies, pray for them, and even do good to them. This ministry is not a reflexive response to their goodness to you; there is no goodness. It is not based on their positive response to you. They're your enemies; they want the worst for you; that's why they're called enemies.

A proactive ministry has its basis in your knowledge of the need of another person. That person may be an enemy, a friend, or a stranger. Because you can't be responsible for everyone, God shows you the particular people He wants you to help. There is some latitude here for the masses of the world. You must rely on God to lead you to needy people because you may not know who they are.

But you do know who your mate is, and you can rest assured that God is leading you to minister mercy to his or her needs—not reactively but proactively. You don't show mercy by sitting back and waiting for him to make the first move. So many marriages deteriorate into a "you first" mindset that nobody goes first. A wife says, "I'll submit when you love me," while the husband protests, "I'll love you when you submit!" Everybody loses in this arrangement. Who is going to start this thing?

Many think that it is a sign of weakness to move first. They see evidence of strength in holding out the longest. Even a pastor once told me that he saw his role as responding to requests for help rather than offering them voluntarily, even if he suspected a person was in need. This, to him, was a test of their desperation and sincerity. It might be a good test of the sincerity or desperation of the suffering one, but it is a poor test for mercy.

"Brethren, if a man be overtaken in a fault, ye which are spiritual, restore such an one in the spirit of meekness" (Gal. 6:1). *"As we have therefore opportunity, let us do good unto all men, especially unto them who are of the household of faith"* (Gal. 6:10). The apostle is teaching that you should take the initiative, not wait on the cries for help of those in despair.

It is always the response of the "spiritual" person to move toward the feeble, the sick, and the needy. The Lord Jesus saw a man who was crippled for thirty-eight years lying by the pool of Bethesda. It was considered a place of healing because of the seasonal appearance of an angel who healed the first to enter the water, which he would stir. Jesus approached the man and asked him if he wanted to be healed. The man explained that he wanted to be healed but someone else always preceded him into the water. Upon hearing this, the Lord healed him on the spot (John 5). Please notice that Jesus approached the man uninvited. The man did not ask Him for help. Christ inquired as to his need and then met it. This is the spiritual response that the Galatians 6 passage is addressing. When a person is spiritual, he shows it by his sensitivity to the needs of others, by a desire to help them. *We then that are strong ought to bear the infirmities of the weak, and not to please ourselves*" (Rom. 15:1).

Who knows the needs of your mate better than you do? Who has a better opportunity to help than you do? Whom has God chosen for this task other than you?

DOCTRINAL RESTRAINT

I was counseling a couple when the husband unleashed one of the most abusive diatribes imaginable against all the failures and shortcomings of his poor wife, who was listening in obvious pain. When I interrupted him, he glared at me, grunted, and sat back stiffly with a smug, look of self-righteous superiority. "You feel very good right now, don't you?" I asked. "Yes, I do!" he replied. "Why is that?" I inquired. "Well, brother," he intoned, "I take pride in telling it like it is! I'm an honest man, and I think a man should say what's on his mind!" "Yes," I replied slowly, "the Bible discusses that very viewpoint: *A fool uttereth all his mind: but a wise man keepeth it in till afterward*'" (Prov. 29:11). To his credit, he came to see his error and repented. This man was obviously not at all concerned about his wife's feelings or her needs. He desired only to feel better about himself. He held nothing back and then compounded the problem by calling evil good. He had not learned the value of "doctrinal restraint."

"Doctrinal restraint" is a term I use to describe the practice of withholding any information for which the listener is not prepared or which may hurt him in some way.

"The secret things belong unto the Lord our God" (Deut. 29:29). God doesn't tell us everything. There are some "secrets" reserved unto Himself alone. Maybe it's because He desires to protect us from knowing too much. The Lord Jesus Christ told His disciples that there were some things He could not tell them because they just weren't able to handle them: *"I have yet many things to say unto you, but ye cannot bear them now"* (John 16:12).

The apostle Paul wrote to the church at Corinth and let them know that he had to adapt his words to them to fit their spiritual immaturity: *"And I, brethren, could not speak unto you as unto spiritual, but as unto carnal, even as unto babes in Christ. I have fed you with milk, and not with meat: for hitherto ye were not able to bear it, neither yet now are ye able. For ye are yet carnal"* (I Cor. 3:1–3).

Merciful communication in marriage means to share truth with your mate to accommodate his particular perception and not to harm in any way. It is an action that is tempered with the knowledge of its effect on the hearer.

No parents with any sensitivity would discuss an impending bankruptcy in their car with their children in the back seat. They want to protect those little ears and hearts from too much information. What is true of children is also true of adults. The speaker should always consider the needs of the listener before sharing too much truth. The truth has to be restrained to fit the individual. This is "doctrinal restraint." Here are some ways to practice doctrinal restraint.

Express Your Pain as Hurt Instead of Anger

First, protect your spouse by expressing your pain as personal hurt instead of projected anger. It's one thing to say, "That really hurt me when you said that, Honey." It's another to scream, "What do you mean saying that? Of all the unkind and stupid things to say, that takes the cake!" Both statements reflect pain, but the statement of hurt states the facts in such a way that the listener is not hurt. The holding back of emotions has protected him.

Men are especially prone to fail in this area. It's not macho to talk about hurt and pain, so we throw things and exert our masculinity. We raise our voices and tear into our mate. Of course, we don't stop to think about the repercussions of all this. We just want to feel better. In the meantime, though, our wives are being bruised and bloodied by this frontal attack. *"Grievous words stir up anger"* (Prov. 15:1) and this type of conversation is ripe for the stirring. Even if you are angry as a husband, the emotion behind the anger is often pain. Far better to express it as a pain, for your wife's protection, than to vent it to her harm. Your wife is not turned off by your transparency and honesty. It endears you to her. Sharing your pain as a genuine hurt not only says, "I trust you with this knowledge," but also says, "I don't want to hurt you in any way."

In our counseling, we have a rule: "You can express your feelings as long as there are not undue feelings in your expression." It's one thing to say, "I'm feeling angry." It's another to throw things against the wall. Discuss them but don't expose them. Say it, but don't display it.

Express Pain as Perception Instead of Accusation

Another way of practicing doctrinal restraint in your conversation is to always express your pain as personal and perceptual instead of to attack the character or motive of your mate. It's okay to say, "When you criticize me, I feel that you are rejecting me as a person, and that hurts." This is far different from saying, "You are such a critic. All you ever do is criticize me. I think you enjoy it when you hurt me." Very hurtful words indeed and damaging to the marriage. Far better to protect the feelings of your mate and protect the future of your relationship.

ALLOW TIME TO "WARM UP" TO AN IDEA

Thirdly, realize that one partner may be able to flatfoot the creek while the other needs a quarter of a mile to build up a head of steam. Usually, the man can stand on one side of the creek, put both feet together and, with a grunt, jump it flatfooted. The wife, on the other hand, may not be so aggressive. She may need some time to adjust to this creek jumpin' business.

I recall coming home on a Sunday evening after church, greeting my wife, "Guess what, honey! Thirty teenagers are coming over for pizza in a few minutes. Won't that be fun." I had just flatfooted the creek, but my dazed wife wasn't with me. She got through it like the trooper she is, but I learned that she did not view the creek like I did. She needs to walk up to the creek, examine it carefully for the speed of the current, the depth of the water, the launching site, and the far shore. She wants to walk the shoreline studying these things and asking some hard questions about the pH level, the presence of critters, and the hidden rocks. She needs to see if there is any moss on the rock from which she is jumping. Then she can back up about two hundred yards or so, paw the ground a bit, and take off like the wind.

Now, I can either push her to hurry up, or I can bide my time for her sake, take her by the hand, and run together with her and jump as one. There was a time when I would face a major decision by praying over it, mulling over it, getting counsel about it, then making the decision and announcing it to my startled wife.

Wives are often more security conscious than their conquest-oriented husbands are. While men focus on the adventure of a new undertaking and the challenge it represents to them, the wives may be reflecting on the loss of the children's friends, redecorating a new home, getting established again in another church, and so forth. I have learned to give Sandra time to acclimate to a new idea, express her concerns, and ask her heartfelt questions. I let her point out the flaws in my logic, partly to hear her viewpoints (and she has some good ones) and partly to exercise restraint by staying in sync with her needs while we cross the creek.

ACCEPT YOUR MATE'S FEELINGS AS LEGITIMATE

I was once visiting in a pastor's home when he and his wife asked if they could get my counsel. The man told me a heart-wrenching story of childhood abuse and neglect. He put his face in his hands and wept bitterly for several minutes. He seemed fearful of my seeing him like this, so I said, "It's okay to cry." I hugged him and prayed with him. He later told me that those simple words told him that I understood. Is it okay to cry? Some think not. But tears are a legitimate outlet for the pain in our heart. Is it okay to cry all day every day for twenty years? Of course not. But let's not assume that twenty minutes of crying equals twenty years of self-pity. Such confusion contributes to a hesitancy in accepting your mate's feelings as legitimate. Here are some other reasons it's difficult for some to accept these feelings.

TO ACCEPT THEM IS TO CONDONE THEM

For our purposes, let's consider the emotion of depression. There is a fear in some as they look at their mate's "illogical" depression. "If I accept these feelings, does my mate think that I'm condoning the validity of them?" If you think the feelings are silly or unjustified, does accepting them not signal to your mate that you condone the sinfulness or ignorance behind them? Is it possible to accept a person's depression without condoning the sin (if sin exists) in that depression? Luke 24 records the story of the Lord Jesus and two very depressed men. He knew they were discouraged and asked them why they were sad. He listened to them carefully as they walked on the road to Emmaus. Did He condone the sinful thinking behind their depression? Not on your life. A cursory reading of the chapter will dispel such a notion. Our Lord had a reason for this accommodation of their sadness, as we shall see in a moment.

IT NEGATES OUR RIGHT TO BE ANGRY WITH THEM

Let's admit it; there are times when we enjoy our anger; and of course, everyone knows the fault lies with our mate and his insensitive actions. "If he hurt me, then I'm going to hurt him. After all, I have a right to hurt someone because I've been hurt." (Strange, it never occurs to us that if we have the right to justify our anger because of hurt, maybe our mate has the same right.) "But now I'm supposed to look at this spouse of mine and accept these feelings? That's not fair. If I accept the feelings that have made me so angry as legitimate, doesn't that mean I can't be angry anymore? That's no fun!" Many people, especially angry people, simply refuse to accept their partner's right to have these feelings because they would have to forfeit their own anger.

TO ACCEPT A FEELING ENCOURAGES THE PERMANENCY OF THAT FEELING

Some people fear that to accept a mate's right to feel depressed will encourage them to embrace that depression permanently, a horrible thought indeed. Christ did not feel this way with the depressed duo in Luke 24. He saw the acceptance of the men's feeling as a means of understanding the beliefs behind those feelings, and that was key to His treatment of their depression.

WE FAIL TO RECOGNIZE FEELINGS AS A STARTING PLACE FOR REAL CHANGE

When Christ asked the men why they were sad, He had a plan all along. He wanted to identify the belief that had generated their depression. We know that the head moves the heart and the heart moves the hand. Christ listened for the lies that had led to this abject depression. When He found them, He corrected them, explaining from the Scriptures why the Christ should have suffered and been glorified. When He left them, their hearts "burned" within them, and they were beside themselves with joy. The Lord had seen the feelings as a starting place for change. He reached into the shadows of their sorrow to take their hand and to lead them into the sunlight of truth.

In my counseling, I use the "ABCs of FEELINGS." It looks like this:

A—ACTIVATING EVENT interpreted by the
B—BELIEF SYSTEM that causes
C—CONSEQUENTIAL FEELINGS that produces
D—DECISIVE BEHAVIOR

A wife came to me in depression on one occasion. When I showed her this chart and asked her to explain her depression with it, she explained it like this: the activating event was an argument with her husband that triggered her belief system that God was punishing her for her past sins by giving her a husband to purge her of those sins. So her belief system revealed a low view of God, a poor view of her husband, and a misunderstanding of marriage as well. This led to consequential feelings of depression that then resulted in a decisive behavior of curling up in the fetal position and staying in bed for two to three days at a time. I used the chart to show her that her feelings were a window to her true beliefs. It gave me, as her counselor, a means of examining the beliefs that needed correcting for a long-term change in her life. Feelings then should be valued as a starting place for lasting change. This certainly helps in the acceptance of them as legitimate. Just as Christ accepted the feelings of the men in Luke 24 as a means of helping them, so we should see feelings of a mate as a means of ministry.

We Fail to Look Beyond Faults to See Needs

As a child, I perceived my father as a hard-boiled ex-marine. He was nondemonstrative and rarely expressed affection to me in any form. I assumed by this he didn't care much for me.

Years passed, and my perception lingered, so much so that as an adult I restricted my visits to his home to overnight.

Imagine my surprise when, while observing me pack the trunk of my car one time, he said somewhat gruffly, "When are you ever going to stay longer than one night?"

In his own way, Dad was saying what I wanted to hear. As a child I would have heard the tone of his voice and concluded that he didn't care. As an adult I could look beyond the tone of his voice and hear the need of his heart.

If it were ever true that man looks on the outward appearance, it is when we fail to look beyond faults to see needs. It takes a special measure of mercy here to look at an angry sullen teenager and see past that armor to the vulnerable, hurting child inside. Such hardness puts us off if we are not careful and cancels any viable ministry. Most people have acquired a long-standing practice of hiding their true feelings behind one mask or another for self-protection. If we focus only on the mask, we fail to accept the feelings behind the mask. A merciful mate will learn to get beneath the surface to the real person hiding there. Learning to look "on the heart" is a major step toward Christlikeness and a ministry of mercy.

Conclusion

The reason for the success of the Love Thy Neighbor Banquet is the same reason that merciful communication produces successful marriages: actions demonstrate real love.

Christian marriage isn't merely reacting to difficulties with grace; it's acting to change those circumstances with mercy. *"Be not overcome of evil, but overcome evil with good"* (Rom. 12:21). The ultimate way of overcoming evil in a marriage relationship is the good of active mercy.

16

How Do I Forgive?

Abroken-hearted wife who sat across from me had recently learned that her husband had been unfaithful. She looked deeply into my eyes and through her tears she asked, "Brother Binney, I know I am supposed to forgive, but *how* do I forgive?" Like a flaming arrow this question pierced my heart. I had never been asked this before. I had counseled many on the need of forgiveness but never on the actual method involved. This hurting wife wanted to know how to translate her obligation into action.

Probably no other relationship is as rife with potential for anger as is marriage. It is the only human relationship in which a man and woman are thrown together for a lifetime in such transparent proximity. This does not allow hiding any weaknesses or impressing one another like one can a stranger. There are no secrets. Marriage exposes both partners to the pressure of stressful moments. It is fertile soil for emotional differences and a culture dish to breed the germs of anger and unforgiveness.

You may not have experienced the sting of adultery in your marriage, but there are many other things that can plant the seeds of bitterness. Over the years that bitterness can germinate and burst into full view with poisonous effects. This woman had shown great maturity and wisdom in seeking help early when the discovery was fresh.

As I reflected on her question, I was convicted. If it is true that *"to him that knoweth to do good, and doeth it not, to him it is sin"* (James 4:17), then to tell a person to do good without showing him how he may do it can contribute to his guilt. Had I inadvertently added to this dear wife's burden? The thought of it drove me to my knees. I often go to my knees when counseling, primarily to pray "the counselor's prayer"— "Lord, what in the world do I tell this woman?" (I pray that prayer a lot, by the way.)

God directed my attention immediately to a passage of Scripture I had read often but had failed to apply to this situation. *"Forbearing one another, and forgiving one another, if any man have a quarrel against any: even as Christ forgave you, so also do ye"* (Col. 3:13). I was immediately struck with the phrase *"even as Christ forgave you, so also do ye."* "This is it!" I thought to myself. "This is the key to forgiveness!" I'm not really sure why that should have surprised me; after all, the essence of the Christian life is to be like Christ. The Scriptures clearly declare that *"as he is, so are we in this world"* (I John 4:17).

Christ is the supreme example of life and living. He is our example of humility and service to others. *"If I then, your Lord and Master, have washed your feet; ye also ought to wash one another's feet"* (John 13:14). He is our pattern of personal holiness. *"As he . . . is holy, so be ye holy in all manner of conversation"* (I Pet. 1:15). He is our model for love. *"Walk in love as Christ also hath loved us"* (Eph. 5:2). How normal and right it is, then, that He should be the model of our forgiveness.

The key to forgiveness is to understand how Christ forgave and to emulate these things in our own heart and marriage. How did He forgive? There is no greater picture of our Lord's forgiveness than the cross of Calvary. Let's go there to see how He forgave.

He Suffered for the Sins of Others

It is generally understood that we must suffer as a consequence of our own sins. However, the thought of suffering for the sins of others is abhorrent and contrary to every fiber of our natural man. But it was this very thing that was at the heart of Christ's willingness to forgive us.

The record of Scripture is clear: the reason Jesus Christ went to the cross is that He intended to suffer vicariously in our place to take the punishment of our sins upon Himself. *"And you, being dead in your sins and the uncircumcision of your flesh, hath he quickened together with him, having forgiven you all trespasses; blotting out the handwriting of ordinances that was against us, which was contrary to us, and took it out of the way, nailing it to his cross"* (Col. 2:13–14).

In the days in which this was written, it was the rule of Roman law that if a man committed crimes, these offenses were to be written on a document. That document would then be nailed to the door of his prison cell until he had served his time and paid the penalty for all his offenses. The laws or "ordinances" he had violated were there in plain sight for all to see. Since the document was in handwritten form, it was called the "handwriting of ordinances" against the prisoner.

When the prisoner had completed his sentence, the document was taken off his prison door. The magistrate would write across it "It is finished" and return it to the prisoner as proof that he had paid his debt to society. If he were challenged on the street, he merely produced the document as evidence that he was clear and had a right to his freedom.

The picture here of our Lord is beautiful indeed! He is seen traversing the long prison hallway that stretches from history past to eternity future. It houses every prisoner of sin that ever lived, representing every sin ever imagined or practiced by wicked flesh. He begins His journey, pausing outside every cell door, your cell door, and rips the document off your door. He continues His journey, pausing at door after door until He has collected every single paper. He then takes it out of the prison, carries it to the cross, and nails it there. He then sheds His precious blood to pay for all that sin, crying out, "It is finished!"

So you see, Christ forgave by suffering for the sins of others. But more to the point, dear friend, He suffered for your sin. *"Surely he hath borne our griefs, and carried our sorrows. . . . he was wounded for our transgressions, he was bruised for our iniquities: the chastisement of our peace was upon him; and with his stripes we are healed. . . . the Lord hath laid on him the iniquity of us all"* (Isa. 53:4–6).

I fear we sometimes lose the significance of this in looking at the bigger picture of Christ dying for the sins of all mankind. Yes, He did die for all the sins of all the world for all time. But to lose sight of the fact that it was your sins that put Him there is to lose something very precious indeed. Tozer comments on this passage in Isaiah with these piercing words.

> A great shadow lies upon every man and every woman—the fact that our Lord was bruised and wounded and crucified for the entire human race. This is the basic human responsibility that men are trying to push off and evade.
>
> Let us not eloquently blame Judas nor Pilate. Let us not curl our lips at Judas and accuse, "He sold Him for money!"
>
> Let us pity Pilate, the weak-willed, because he did not have courage enough to stand for the innocency of the man whom he declared had done no wrong.
>
> Let us not curse the Jews for delivering Jesus to be crucified. Let us not single out the Romans in blaming them for putting Jesus on the cross.
>
> Oh, they were guilty, certainly! But they were our accomplices in crime. They and we put Him on the cross, not they alone. That rising malice and anger that burns so hotly in your breast today put Him there. That basic dishonesty that comes to light in your being when you knowingly cheat and chisel on your income tax return—that put Him on the cross. The evil, the hatred, the suspicion, the jealousy, the lying tongue, the carnality, the fleshly love of pleasure—all of these in natural man joined in putting Him on the cross.
>
> We may as well admit it. Every one of us in Adam's race had a share in putting Him on the cross![1]

Now it gets personal; just as Jesus suffered for the sinfulness of other men, He calls upon us to do the same. *"Remember the word that I said unto you, The servant is not greater than his lord. If they have persecuted me, they will also persecute you"* (John 15:20). Clearly then, it is a calling of the Christian life to suffer persecution: *"Yea, and all that will live godly in Christ Jesus shall suffer persecution"* (II Tim. 3:12).

Furthermore, Jesus makes it clear that this suffering is something that is modeled by Him. His willingness to suffer as a result of man's sinfulness is not limited to Him but is to be emulated by His followers. *"Let this mind be in you, which was also in Christ Jesus: who . . . humbled himself, and became obedient unto death, even the death of the cross"* (Phil. 2:5–8).

To fail to have the mind of Christ reveals a gross misunderstanding of the Master-servant relationship we share with Christ. What He endured, we must endure. To refuse to do so, or to think it unfair, is the height of arrogance and bespeaks the corruption of pride: *"The servant is not greater than his lord"* (John 13:16).

What causes a person whose sins nailed Christ to the cross and who rejoices in His merciful forgiveness to turn from the cross with anger toward another? What prompts him to find a fellow sinner who has offended him in a far lesser way and refuse to forgive him? What causes a husband to accept God's forgiveness of his sins and reject God's command to forgive his wife? What causes a wife to rejoice that her hunger for forgiveness has been met but to relish the starvation of a husband whose affront she will not let go? Can it be pride? Can it be the unspoken manifestation of thinking somehow that they are greater than their Lord?

What they are saying is "Thank you, sinless Lamb of God, for suffering for my sins, for the sinfulness of others, *but don't ask me to do the same.*"

The opinion of God about such posturing is clear from even a casual reading of Matthew 18:21–35. The story is told of a servant who was forgiven for an enormous debt owed to his master—estimates range as high as a million dollars in today's currency. He turns around and finds a fellow servant who owed him a measly $15. Because the fellow servant could not pay, he threw him into debtor's prison until he made the debt good. When the master heard of this, he called the insensitive servant before him. *"O thou wicked servant, I forgave thee all that debt . . .*

shouldest not thou also have had compassion on thy fellowservant, even as I had pity on thee? And his lord was wroth, and delivered him to the tormentors, till he should pay all that was due unto him" (Matt. 18:32–34). Then follows a solemn warning from the Lord Jesus Himself, *"So likewise shall my heavenly Father do also unto you, if ye from your hearts forgive not every one his brother their trespasses"* (v. 35).

Can it be that the greater sin is that of refusing to forgive after being forgiven? Is that why the wrath of the master was directed toward the servant?

Perhaps you, like the woman who asked how to forgive, have been the victim of the sinfulness of your mate. If you could get on one of the TV talk shows and tell your story, you would likely get a lot of sympathy. In fact, you would probably find that the crowd would urge you on in your unswerving devotion to bitterness and your determination to get revenge. But that doesn't make it right. You could go out to a mall parking lot, line up one thousand people, tell them your story, and probably convince them all to agree that you have every right to be angry. But don't put Jesus in the line!

Suffering because of the sinfulness of others is a staple of Bible expectations for the believer. In fact, one is hard-pressed to identify any human suffering that is not traceable, directly or indirectly, to the wickedness of another human being . . . even if you have to go all the way back to the Garden of Eden.

It is not enough, however, to merely acknowledge that you will be mistreated, that this is part of the Christian existence. Such passive or even reluctant admission doesn't demand a willingness to suffer for another. It is this willingness of Christ that John addresses in I John 3:16: *"Hereby perceive we the love of God, because he laid down his life for us: and we ought to lay down our lives for the brethren."* In this statement, John extends the theme of persecution to that of a willingness to suffer for another's transgressions.

How Do I Forgive?

The beginning of Christlike forgiveness is to emulate His willingness to forgive from His heart the suffering imposed upon Him by the acts of sinful men. Yes, you may have suffered in your marriage; you may have even suffered because of your marriage partner, but no one was ever more of a victim than our Lord Jesus Christ Himself, and His willingness to be a victim is ours to copy and the key to our own forgiving.

He Prayed for His Enemies

Christ met with His disciples and uttered these penetrating words: *"I say unto you, Love your enemies, bless them that curse you, do good to them that hate you, and pray for them which despitefully use you, and persecute you"* (Matt. 5:44). These were not hollow platitudes uttered by our Lord. They were not the pontifications of some armchair theologian whose hands had never been dirtied by contact with the real world. This was His practice, vividly illustrated on the cross when He prayed, *"Father, forgive them; for they know not what they do"* (Luke 23:34). Within this poignant prayer there are key ingredients, transforming principles that made His prayer such a powerful model for you!

He Appealed to God on Their Behalf

When the Lord Jesus prayed that prayer, He, more than anyone else, knew the depth of the need of His malefactors. He had experienced firsthand the sting of their venom. It was their wrath that drove them, their hatred that condemned Him. It was their hands that bound Him and bruised Him. It was their demon-crazed eyes into which He was gazing when He prayed. It was their sin that nailed Him to the cross; and it was over the crescendo of a cacophony of mocking voices amidst raised fists and shrieks for His blood that His prayer was lifted to heaven.

It is precisely because Christ had experienced these things that He was best qualified to pray for His enemies. Think about it. In that crowd were the Pharisees and Sadducees, the highly respected and honored spiritual leaders of the nation. Their hearts were full of envy and hatred, and yet to all outward appearances they epitomized holiness and reverence. Why would their followers be motivated to pray for them? Jesus knew better. He had felt the lash of their blood lust and He knew what was in man. So He prayed.

Who better to pray for your enemy, even if you consider your mate to be your enemy, than you, the eyewitness of his failure, you who have tasted firsthand the dregs of his depravity? Who could possibly be motivated more to pray for his needs than you, the person that God has allowed to see the aching greatness of those needs? It would certainly not be the people at church who tell you how impressed they are with your mate's spirituality, not the people who see your husband in a key role of spiritual leadership, not the congregation who watches your pious wife singing in the choir. Why not? Because God didn't call them to pray for their friends as much as He called you to pray for your enemy.

This is a high and holy calling, a sacred trust from God. To pray under the sovereign placement of this person into your life, to pray from a knowledge of need, to pray out of a burden of pain is the ultimate opportunity to intercede for another with purpose. This is not merely a divine commission, it is also the outworking of a divine plan.

It is more than an opportunity; it is a holy responsibility. But it is a responsibility that many people have shirked. They have justified this neglect on the basis of their pain, the unfairness of it all, the evil of their enemy, or their need of revenge. But they have shirked it nonetheless. Someone whom God designated for special prayers is not getting them. Someone whose hope lay in their specially assigned intercessor has lost that hope because that intercessor rejected their commission. I wonder, if the truth were known, how many souls are limping through life in the bondage of sin simply because some person failed to pray for them.

Thank God that the ministry Christ began on Calvary is still being carried on today. He ever liveth to make intercession for us. And He calls on you to do the same for your mate.

17

THE MINISTRY OF SEXUALITY

And David comforted Bathsheba his wife, and went in
unto her, and lay with her.
II Samuel 12:24

By any standards, the ancient city of Corinth represented the worst of immorality and sexual decadence. As the home of Venus worship, it was notorious, even in the pagan world, for its wantonness. In fact its very name became synonymous with sin; to "corinthianize" meant to practice the extremes of moral perversions. Over five hundred thousand people inhabited a city known for its beauty and opulence, many of them drawn there by the singular promise of unrestrained wickedness.

It was to this city that God led the apostle Paul to establish one of the early churches. In the year and a half he labored there, he won many of its citizens to Christ—some from the lower classes, some from the higher, but all immersed in the carnal culture surrounding them, many of them saved out of a reprehensible past of unrestrained immorality.

In reaction to this and out of a sincere but erroneous belief that sexual abstinence produced spiritual superiority, some had felt it best not to marry, while others who were married thought it better to set themselves apart wholly for God by sacrificing the sexual relationship. This arose partly from the view that the body and its natural instincts are intrinsically evil and therefore to be avoided and partly from the view that sex is primarily self-gratifying and self-serving. Paul addressed these errors by underscoring the need of seeing sex in the context of ministry to your spouse. *"Let the husband render unto the wife due benevolence:*

and likewise also the wife unto the husband. The wife hath not power of her own body, but the husband: and likewise also the husband hath not power of his own body, but the wife" (I Cor. 7:3–4).

Today, the Christian marriage faces some of the same issues. A common tendency among the overzealous is to allow the pendulum of behavior to swing wildly from one extreme to the other, from loose immorality to repressive spirituality, from license to legalism. A person saved out of a wicked past may avoid any relationship or activity that reminds him of his past sinfulness.

On the other hand, a carnal Christian, still under the influence of the past, may bring into marriage the view that sex serves solely as a means of personal pleasure rather than compassionate ministry.

It is to both groups that Paul emphasizes the need to render unto their mates the goodness that is due them by satisfying their sexual needs, not from a motive of manipulation but from one of ministry.

It is essential to approach this crucial part of marriage with the understanding that you are not to come to the marriage bed to get but to give, not to be ministered unto but to minister. As long as self-gratification and selfish pleasure are the primary motivation for sex, you will never enjoy God's full blessings. You may pray earnestly for more excitement in your intimate life but not realize it if "*ye ask amiss, that ye may consume it upon your lusts*" (James 4:3).

This was the apostle's purpose in his writing. He desired to establish a goal of mutual ministry and deferential consideration in marital sexuality, stressing the need to always place your mate's needs above your own.

This thinking is foreign to most Christians of our day; in fact, it is such a radical departure from the modern, culturally driven view of sex that some will find it difficult to embrace. "Sexual ministry" sounds like an oxymoron to them. "How can it be sex and be a ministry too?" they ask. "Ministry" has a spiritual tone to it, even a holy connotation. The fact that sex is so far removed from the spiritual may have more to do with our own pasts than with God's Word. It may be a reflection of our own corrupted worldview. Like the Corinthians of old, many of today's Christians need to shed the graveclothes of the past and acquire a biblical conviction about the need of using their sexuality as a means of ministering to their mate.

David understood this. After his adultery with Bathsheba, a baby was born to them, but it lived only seven days. To his credit, David immediately went to the house of the Lord and worshiped. After he had communed with God, he made his way to his house and his wife.

Bathsheba certainly had her own grief to deal with; there was the weight of her guilt and effects of her sin, but there was more—a mother's knowledge that her sin had been the cause of her baby's death. For a mother to lose a child is in itself a grievous burden to bear, but with all things considered, she bore a wound that almost defied healing. That is, until her husband came home from his time with God. Because he had been comforted, he was able to comfort her, and because he knew that she needed a sexual ministry, he met her need: *"And David comforted Bathsheba his wife, and went in unto her, and lay with her"* (II Sam. 12:24).

With the glow of God's presence still clinging to him, David went from the church to the marriage bed. He saw one to be as spiritual as the other.

This is the view of sexuality that is needed by Christian couples today. It is eminently spiritual to engage in the sexual act; it is the will of God, it pleases Him, it can be done even in the spirit of temple prayers, and it ministers to your mate. What a difference such a conviction would bring to many marriages. But how is this spiritual worldview acquired? How does one change his perceptions of sexuality after years of thinking in the opposing vein?

The answer is to go back to the basics, to start over by relearning the truth that will set you free. It is needful to unlearn the *"philosophy and vain deceit"* that is *"after the tradition of men, after the rudiments of the world, and not after Christ"* (Col. 2:8). It is necessary to become reeducated in the basic teachings of biblical sexuality.

What is needed is some sound biblical sex education. "What!" I can hear some say. "Everyone knows that sex education is wrong!"

Such thinking is not new. Sex education courses have long been the target of the fiercest attacks of Bible believers. And so they should be. Their inordinate focus on the plumbing and practice of the reproductive system has stirred the lusts of thousands of underdeveloped youth and earned them a permanent niche in perversion's hall of fame.

But if sex education courses aren't the answer, where does a Christian go to learn about sex? When a child asks a parent about that word, does he react in horror? When a teenager wants answers to the problem of his raging hormones, are parents prepared to help him? When a new convert is desperately trying to overcome his licentious past, can he approach the pastor or enroll in a course for help? It seems that more youth are learning about sex from MTV and the locker room than from home or church.

The tragic result of this is that youthful hang-ups become adult dysfunctions. And many young people take their sexual habits, worldviews, sexual perversions, and moral confusion into the marriage chamber.

In an attempt to do battle with the perverted sex educators such as S.I.E.C.U.S., the now debunked Alfred Kinsey, Dr. Ruth, and others, we have thrown the baby out with the bath water. It is not sex education that is wrong; it is the people, methods, and philosophies behind it that are wrong.

But the Bible has much to say on the subject. God talks about sex! After all, He created it. Out of His goodness and love He gave us an instruction manual to help us out.

In the Bible, He gives us some key principles to govern our sexuality. We have a biblical theology of human sexuality far greater than any man's philosophy can provide. There are key doctrines in this theology that every husband and wife need to embrace and celebrate. What are they? To answer that, we will concentrate on Paul's first letter to the Corinthians, chapters 6 and 7, while borrowing from other portions of Scripture.

THE DOCTRINE OF PRESENT VICTORY

"And such were some of you: but ye are washed, but ye are sanctified, but ye are justified in the name of the Lord Jesus, and by the Spirit of our God" (I Cor. 6:11). Paul has spent the first part of this chapter in I Corinthians correcting the practice of taking a brother before a secular court. The basis of this criticism is the depraved nature of the unconverted, which make up the court. What right have they to judge a Christian? They are sexual libertines immersed in fornication, adultery, homosexuality, and so forth.

To underscore the wisdom of a brother's judging a brother, he establishes the believer's credentials. He makes it clear that they, too, were once like their worldly counterparts, but they have been changed. *"Such were some of you."* He uses three words to describe this change: *"washed,"* *"sanctified,"* and *"justified."*

Washed is a reference to their new life in Christ. They are saved *"by the washing of regeneration"* (Titus 3:5). They are *"new creatures"* now.

Sanctified, meaning to be set apart for God's use, reminds the new convert of his new behavior as a follower of Christ. Being set apart for God did not allow the sinful practices of the past, and these Corinthians knew it.

Justified is a word Paul uses to remind them of their new standing in Christ and before God. A major motivation behind sexual bondage is the need for acceptance. Sadly, temporary or even fantasized intimacy displaces real intimacy, and the drive is often a need of acceptance.

But nobody ever feels totally accepted apart from being *"accepted in the beloved"* (Eph. 1:6). It is in this acceptance in God that Paul urges the Corinthians to glory. "You have it all!" Paul seems to say. "You have a new life, a new behavior, and a new standing. You have victory over your past."

And so do you, dear friend. If the New Testament teaches anything, it is the profound truth of our victory over sin. This is not something to work toward but to work from. It is not a goal of the Christian life as much as it is the foundation from which we seek to achieve higher goals. *"Such were some of you."* We are declared to be *"dead to sin"* and *"alive unto God."* Paul is emphatic when he writes, *"Our old man is crucified with him, that the body of sin might be destroyed,"* and continues this thought, *"likewise reckon ye also yourselves to be dead indeed unto sin, but alive unto God through Christ Jesus our Lord"* (Rom. 6:6, 11).

The first doctrine of a theology of sexuality that a Christian must embrace is that sin no longer has dominion over you, and you should *"let not sin . . . reign in your mortal body"* (Rom. 6:12). Notice the word *"let."* It is your choice to allow your past to blind you to your future. It is your choice to extend your hands for Satan to cuff. You must stop lying down and playing dead when sin rears its ugly head. *"Know ye not, that to whom ye yield yourselves servants* [slaves] *to obey, his servants ye are to whom ye obey; whether of sin unto death, or of obedience unto righteousness?"* (Rom. 6:16). The way is clear. You *do* have a choice. It is time to stop believing the *"accuser,"* the *"father of lies,"* who has worked overtime to convince you that you don't stand a chance.

St. Augustine was one of the most brilliant minds in the history of the church. Before he became a great leader for God, he was a rising star of the pagan world. He was well on his way to fame as an orator and philosopher. But in his *Confessions of St. Augustine*, he reveals that he was also one of the greatest sinners alive, morally profligate and sexually promiscuous to the extreme. He saw no way of victory. But when he was saved, he was enabled to cleanse his life of his wicked past. One day, while he was walking down the street, one of his former mistresses called out, "Augustine! It is I!" Augustine kept walking, ignoring her call. "Augustine," she cried, "Augustine, it is I." No response from Augustine. Finally, she came alongside and looked him in the face. "Augustine," she insisted, "it is I!" "Yes," said Augustine, "but it is *not* I!" and kept on walking. He had learned the truth of his victory over a sinful past.

DOCTRINE OF WHOLESOME SEX

A common obstacle to a quality, intimate life in the marriage is a worldview of "dirty sex." Many men struggle with what I call the "decency factor." Because of carnal exposure to sex, from their first furtive glances at pornography to ultimate moral bondage, they equate sex with sin, women as sex "objects," and pleasure with perverted fantasy. Then they marry a woman of purity and virtue—unlike all the women of their past. She represents all that the other women do not. Now, to enter into something "dirty" with this pure creature creates strong ambivalence. They have hit the wall of the "decency factor" and they are confused. At this point, they often resort to regressive mental fantasies to get them through the sexual experience, attempt to get their wife to cross the wall to their side of perverted practices, shut down in their marriage intimacy, or return to what they're comfortable with, namely "dirty sex."

What is the answer? No man will ever thoroughly enjoy intimacy until he learns to view it as God views it—as "good." It is a pure, wholesome, godly, and spiritual relationship.

The reasons for seeing sex as good are plenteous:

- Almost every book in the Bible discusses sex to some degree.
- In the first three chapters of Genesis, God called every creation "*good,*" but not until He created the union of a man and woman did he call it "*very good.*"

- God saw only one thing as *"not good."* *"And the Lord God said, It is not good that the man should be alone; I will make him an help meet for him"* (Gen. 2:18).

- The first mention of a truth in Bible interpretation is of great significance in determining the importance of that doctrine. It is noteworthy that the first and second mentions of marriage are in regard to the physical union: *"And God blessed them, and God said unto them, Be fruitful, and multiply, and replenish the earth"* (Gen. 1:28). *"Therefore shall a man leave his father and his mother, and shall cleave unto his wife; and they shall be one flesh. And they were both naked, the man and his wife, and were not ashamed"* (Gen. 2:24–25). The emphasis is fruitfulness, oneness of flesh, and disallowance of shame. Interesting choice of words, don't you think, *"and were not ashamed"*? Apparently God wants us to know that there is nothing shameful about the oneness of marriage. Indeed *"marriage is honourable in all"* (Heb. 13:4). There is a belief abroad that postulates that because of the Fall of man, sex has become sinful. Dr. Ed Wheat counters this, "Some have assumed that the sex act became an unholy practice when sin entered into the world. However, this is ruled out when we see that God's basic counsel on sex in the first chapters of Genesis was repeated by Jesus Christ to the religious leaders of his day."[1] In a direct reference to the oneness of flesh of Genesis, Christ concludes, *"What therefore God hath joined together, let not man put asunder"* (Matt.19:6).

The Victorian purist will find this most incredible of all: God has chosen the sexual union of a man and woman to demonstrate His relationship to the church. That's right! *"For this cause shall a man leave his father and mother, and shall be joined unto his wife, and they two shall be one flesh. This is a great mystery: but I speak concerning Christ and the church"* (Eph. 5:31–32). "Thus, the properly and lovingly executed and mutually satisfying sexual union is God's way of demonstrating to us a great spiritual truth."[2] The truth is of the mystical union of Christ and His bride, the church.

Can anyone, *dare anyone*, suggest, in light of these truths, that sex is anything but holy and beautiful? If it is true that "the hearty and grateful acceptance of our sexuality is an essential step in overcoming lust,"[3] then perhaps there is a need for more Christians to get their theology of sex from the Bible instead of *Playboy*. Then they will be able to fully understand the beauty of sex and grow to overcome illicit lust.

DOCTRINE OF SELF-CONTROL

Paul asserts boldly, *"All things are lawful for me, but I will not be brought under the power of any"* (I Cor. 6:12). He is affirming man's role in sin. His "will not" is a reference to the power of the will to refuse to surrender to base lusts of the flesh. Every human has this ability and this responsibility.

A man in counseling once said to me, "I can't help it! I'm only human!" I told him that the primary thing that distinguishes him from an animal is self-control. Animals don't have it; people do. To surrender to the lie that I can't control myself is to reduce the state of God's creation to that of a lower beast.

Self-control is a protection for the believer against becoming a moral *"castaway."* *"But I keep under my body, and bring it into subjection: lest that by any means, when I have preached to others, I myself should be a castaway"* (I Cor. 9:27).

You *do* have self-control. You *must* practice self-control. This is a basic doctrine of the Christian life and is especially meaningful to the married life. It is upon this foundation of personal responsibility and ability that any theology of sex is built. It is time for Christians to exchange a phrase in their sin-enabling vocabulary: "I can't" needs to be replaced with "I won't." No believer can honestly say, "I can't" when the Scriptures declare, *"I can do all things through Christ"* (Phil. 4:13). No child of God can excuse his failure when we are told, *"This is the victory that overcometh the world, even our faith"* (I John 5:4). No one can blame the Devil *"because greater is he that is in you, than he that is in the world"* (I John 4:4). Paul said, *"I will not be brought under the power of any"* and so must you. Only when this doctrine is added to your theology of sexuality will you experience the power and victory of God.

DOCTRINE OF DESIGN

"Now the body is not for fornication, but for the Lord; and the Lord for the body" (I Cor. 6:13). God has a purpose for your body. He has a plan in its design and a reason for its function. Until you understand this grand principle of design, you will never be fulfilled; for no person can ever be fulfilled who does not find God's purpose for his life and accomplish it. What is God's design, or purpose, for your body?

DOCTRINE OF DESIGN SEEN PHILOSOPHICALLY

God created sex for physical fruitfulness (Gen. 1:28), conjugal fellowship (Gen. 2:24), and a visual illustration of Christ's spiritual intimacy with the church (Eph. 5:31–32). To enhance His purpose and to motivate man to that end, He granted the gift of pleasure to accompany the sexual experience.

Man's design, on the other hand, is often limited to pleasure alone. While satisfaction is the result of subjugating man's purpose to God's, sin is the result of man subjugating God's design to his own. Sin is the natural product of ignoring, lowering, or perverting God's higher design. When pleasure is sought with attitudes or actions that fail to recognize God's design, sex becomes distorted. This is not to say that sex should not be pleasurable. Quite the contrary. But ultimate pleasure springs from obedience and conformity to God's will. *"At thy right hand there are pleasures for evermore"* (Ps. 16:11). But if pleasure is the sole motivation for sex, true fulfillment can never be fully realized.

It is vital, therefore, that every believer conform his or her own ideas about the purposes of sex to those of God. Then, and only then, can he find the fulfillment that comes from accomplishing the purposes for which God created his sexuality and his sexual relationship with his mate.

When the doctrine of design is brought to bear upon the physiological differences between man and woman, it is clear that there is only one interrelation that can accomplish all three purposes. Only one alignment for sexual union accomplishes God's purpose of fruitfulness and fellowship. As Wheat writes, "Let us realize how the bodies of men and women are designed. Even in the sex act itself we are reminded that this is a relationship of persons, not just bodies, for it is no coincidence that man is the *only* creature of God's creation who relates sexually face-to-face."[4]

Even in the third purpose of design, that of illustrating the intimacy of Christ's fellowship with the church, is it not reasonable to assume that God would not stray from His established norm? Can anyone conceive of Christ's holy and spiritual oneness with the church being illustrated by unnatural pornographic practices and methods? At the very least, it falls upon the practitioner of these methods to remove any stigma of doubt from consideration. But the better part of wisdom calls for a defense of God's glory rather than a promotion of man's pleasure.

A vacuum of understanding about God's design for sex, and a fleshly desire to bring variety into the marriage bed, has prompted mankind, even Christian mankind, to resort to the world's philosophies and practices. The quest for pleasure has once again usurped the higher goal of pleasing God, and our marriages have suffered because of it.

I can almost hear the howls of protests from the Christians who have relied upon Hebrews 13:4 as the basis of their sexual philosophy and conduct in marriage. "Hold on now. Doesn't the Bible say that *"marriage is honorable in all, and the bed undefiled"*? And doesn't that mean that as long as you're married, anything goes?"

DOCTRINE OF DESIGN SEEN PRACTICALLY

A common belief among Christians is that as long as an act is confined to the marriage bed, and if both parties are consenting, then it is okay to experiment with a variety of worldly sexual practices. But is that what this verse actually teaches? Is it saying that "anything goes"?

God's design for married sex is honor and purity. His desire is that sexuality reflect the highest and noblest of motives and methods. Hebrews 13:4 is actually teaching the very opposite of what is popularly believed about it. The writer is not saying that because it takes place in marriage that it is unsullied and undefiled. He is not proposing a sanctification of sin by virtue of wedding vows. This is a violent wrenching of the text and a disservice to the sanctity of the Scriptures.

Kenneth Wuest, a highly respected authority on the Greek language, has carefully worded the meaning of the text in this way: "Let your marriage be held in honor in all things, and thus let your marriage bed be undefiled, for whoremongers and adulterers God will judge."⁵ Quite a difference from the popular interpretation. In other words, the fact of marriage in no way precludes the possibility of defiling the bed. Just the opposite. The possibility of defilement is so real that the marriage partners are exhorted to diligently hold the line in their pursuit of holiness.

The primary application of this truth is the emphasis on an exclusive sexual relationship with your marriage partner. It is a call for fidelity to your mate. To fail in this and break the honor of marriage through adultery is to invite the judgment of God. A secondary application would include the practice of ungodly pornographic and perverted variations of the sexual act. What is *pure, lovely*, and *of good report* about this (Phil. 4:8)?

A LACK OF CONTENTMENT

I believe the root problem here is a lack of contentment. God wants us to *"be content with such things as ye have"* (Heb. 13:5), to be content with His design for marriage, to be content with His provision of a marriage partner. But restless mankind wants to try something new. As Tim Stafford writes, "Here we strike at the heart of the problem of lust as the Bible conceives it: We want things that don't belong to us. . . . We are not content with what we have. We want something more—and that desire drives us. Lust shows that, in your heart of hearts, you want somebody else's sexual life. When a man lusts for a woman, he is not grateful for what God has given him."[6] But it goes beyond desiring another woman. It includes the desire for novel experiences. "All sexual sin begins with a desire for someone or some experience that is not rightfully yours."[7]

How does one determine what is "rightfully" his? The answer comes from looking to God's Word and its theology of sexuality, particularly the doctrine of God's design. Do your desires and practices meet His standard?

Every time fleshly tastes are expanded beyond the parameters of God's will, our appetite is enlarged for more because *evil men . . . wax worse and worse*," and one sin leads to another and *"iniquity unto iniquity."* There is no end to the depravity one can reach when once he departs from God's standard of holiness and honor in marriage.

DOCTRINE OF IDENTITY WITH CHRIST

"Know ye not that your bodies are the members of Christ? shall I then take the members of Christ, and make them members of an harlot? God forbid" (I Cor. 6:15). *"Ye are not your own? For ye are bought with a price: therefore glorify God in your body, and in your spirit, which are God's"* (I Cor. 6:19–20). There exists a precious relationship between the believer and Christ, between our bodies and Him. Because our body is His temple and He indwells us, we can no more separate Him from our activities than we can separate ourselves from our own spirit. In fact, we can no more separate ourselves from Him than He can separate Himself from the Godhead. The Bible emphatically declares that an inseparable union exists between the Father, the Son, and the Holy Spirit. *"Hear, O*

Israel: The Lord our God is one Lord" (Deut. 6:4). *"And Jesus answered him, The first of all the commandments is, Hear, O Israel; The Lord our God is one Lord"* (Mark 12:29). Although each person of the Godhead is uniquely one, together they form one God. You cannot separate one from the other. The Lord Jesus Christ reveled in His oneness with the Father and prayed, *"That they may all be one; as thou, Father, art in me, and I in thee"* (John 17:21).

During the sexual union, you become one with your partner, literally becoming *"one flesh"* (Gen. 2:24). This union of two is more than that of two bodies; it is a cleaving, a knowing, a bonding of two personalities much like that of the inseparable union of the Godhead. The Hebrew word translated "one" in Deuteronomy 6:4 and Mark 12:29 quoted above is the same word used to describe the union between sexual partners.

When you understand that *"your bodies are the members of Christ,"* you can understand the reason for the question *"Shall I then take the members of Christ, and make them members of an harlot? God forbid."* But that is exactly what happens when you enter into an immoral sexual union. Christ is a partner with you. He is part of it. You are using part of Christ's body in a sinful way. You place Him in an unthinkable situation.

It is a grievous pain for our Lord to have to endure the desecration of His temple while we engage in sin. Just as the pain of the offended party in adultery is the knowledge that part of him has been given to someone else, so Christ endures pain when His children give themselves to someone else. We are rather to glorify God in our bodies that belong to Him.

Would you be appalled at the notion of someone having sex in your church auditorium? The practice of fornication or adultery is similar. Both violate the sanctity of the sanctuary: one of the church sanctuary, the other of Christ's sanctuary, the body.

We have one identity as Christians. We are not our own; we are God's. We cannot escape this marvelous union. Therefore, we must decide who is in control. Who rules in this body? Paul Tripp confronts this question powerfully: "In the final analysis, human beings live out one of only two identities: that I am ultimate and autonomous or that I am created and dependent on God. . . . In matters of sexuality, the question becomes, Will I live out my identity as a creature of God (. . . a child of God) or will I live as my own god with no higher agenda than my own satisfaction?"[8]

Doctrine of "Flight vs. Fight"

"Flee fornication" (I Cor. 6:18) and *"Flee also youthful lusts"* (II Tim. 2:22). There are some things we are to "resist," there are others we are to "fight," but there are some sins so powerful that we are told to flee them. Sexual sins are among those. Foolish indeed is the youth who attempts to overcome the flesh in a head-on encounter. He will seldom win! God doesn't want you to attack it, but to flee from it. How does one flee from lusts?

One way is to avoid all sources of temptation. *"Enter not into the path of the wicked, and go not in the way of evil men. Avoid it, pass not by it, turn from it, and pass away"* (Prov. 4:14–15). While in the navy, it fell upon me to drive through the "strip" each day going and coming to the base. (Many military bases have a strip, a collection of tawdry places of entertainment that pander to the flesh.) On more than one occasion I got stuck in traffic in the midst of it. There I was, surrounded by porn shops, bars, hookers, and so forth. Trying to think pure thoughts, I was fighting a losing battle. I thought, "There's got to be a better way!" I found another gate in the rear of the base manned by a lone marine. "Can enlisted personnel use this gate?" I asked. "Sure," he said, "but nobody does. This is mainly used for freight deliveries, but you can use it." Although it was out of my way, I found peace of mind and strength of spirit by avoiding that awful strip.

It would have been pure folly to continue to expose myself to the temptations abounding on the strip in a vain attempt to fight the Devil when there was a way to "flee."

An alcoholic doesn't keep a six-pack in the refrigerator to test his resolve, and a sex addict should not expose himself to any temptation— be it a place, a person, or a form of entertainment—that will test him. Flee youthful lusts! For many, even TV can be too much of a fight with its preoccupation with sex and sexual images. Do yourself a favor; pay any price to flee. Don't dance with the Devil! Don't dialogue with the demons! Don't flirt with destruction! Flee! You probably know even now what it is you need to flee. Make a commitment to God to do so.

DOCTRINE OF "SOLE PLEASURE SOURCE"

"To avoid fornication, let every man have his own wife, and let every woman have her own husband" (I Cor. 7:2). There is one and only one source of sexual pleasure for you: your marriage partner. If you are not married, you are forbidden by God to seek such pleasure until you are married. If you are married, you are to restrict such pleasure to your "own wife" or your "own husband," not another's wife or husband.

This also means that man is not to have another source of gratification apart from his mate. Visually, verbally, or physically, your mate is to be your sole means of sexual pleasure. God's Word is clear on this! *"Let thy fountain be blessed: and rejoice with the wife of thy youth. Let her be as the loving hind and pleasant roe; let her breasts satisfy thee at all times; and be thou ravished* [exhilarated] *always with her love"* (Prov. 5:18–19).

It is of note, men, that you are to rejoice with *"the wife of thy youth,"* not "thy youthful wife." When sex is equated with youthfulness instead of fidelity, the enemy will always have a youthful and sensuous alternative. When a girlish figure means more to you than a pure heart and virtuous spirit, you will always have an abundance of temptations; women with such figures are a dime a dozen, but to find a woman with a pure heart, a tender spirit, and a godly countenance is rare indeed. *"Who can find a virtuous woman? for her price is far above rubies"* (Prov. 31:10). *"Virtuous"* is a reference to moral strength. If you have a wife who possesses that, you have indeed found *"a good thing"* (Prov. 18:22).

Shame on the man who marries his wife for her body, then watches her wear that body out in cooking for him, cleaning for him, working to pay the bills for him, and bearing children for him, only to reject her for a fantasy celluloid model or *"strange women"* with whom few wives can compete. No, *"the wife of thy youth"* does not mean youthful wife.

Ladies, whatever else you offer your husband in your old age, it won't be a model's body. But it can be a virtuous heart. Concentrate your time and effort on that which God values. *"Favour is deceitful, and beauty is vain: but a woman that feareth the Lord, she shall be praised"* (Prov. 31:30). Winning your husband through your *"chaste conversation"* will go farther and last longer than prolonged gym workouts that *"profit little."*

DOCTRINE OF LIMITED ABSTINENCE

"Defraud ye not one the other except it be with consent for a time, that ye may give yourselves to fasting and prayer; and come together again" (I Cor. 7:5). It is clear from this verse that neither mate is to deprive the other sexually except under specific conditions: mutual agreement on the matter, a spiritual motive behind the decision, and a carefully limited time frame.

There is no solo decision here, only a consensual one. Both parties must be in harmony about any choices regarding abstinence. For one mate to make this choice alone, even with the best of motives, is to court misunderstanding and to open the door for serious strains within the marriage.

High spiritual motives are assumed to be part of this decision, not self-serving goals or crass agendas. The only spiritual motive the Scripture permits is that of giving yourselves to *"fasting and prayer."*

One of the goals behind fasting is to deprive the flesh of distraction in order to concentrate on spiritual objectives, most notably prayer. Because the flesh thrives on food, many assume that fasting includes only the abstinence from eating. But the flesh's appetite also includes the pleasures of sex. It too can be distracting from spiritual objectives. Therefore, it is included in the process of fasting and prayer. But spiritual fasting is the only reason given here for *"defrauding,"* or depriving, one another.

Even then, there is a careful limitation on the amount of time involved: *"for a time . . . come together again."* There is no question as to the reason for this injunction. Paul makes it clear that to withhold yourselves from one another for too long of a time sets you up for a loss of control, *"incontinency,"* that in turn makes you vulnerable to satanic temptations.

The God-given biological drives within humanity demand occasional satisfaction. God provides the sanctity of the marriage relationship to accommodate this need. But if this venue is denied for too long a period of time, even for the holy purposes of fasting and prayer, the pent-up pressures begin to exert their influence on the individual's self-control. He becomes more susceptible to temptations and more inclined to satisfy his need illegitimately. This is a down time of personal spiritual vulnerability. Enter Satan. It is noteworthy that this is one of the few instances in Scripture that the enemy's influence is attributed to Satan himself. The word here is Satan with a capital "S." The extent of his involvement is not made clear, but it is there. The clear danger, then, in extending this period of sexual abstinence, even with the highest motives, is to set up your marriage for spiritual attack.

Conclusion

Yes indeed, sex education has gotten a bad rap. Its image has been tarnished and denigrated by the touch of unholy hands and polluted minds. History reveals that sex education has been abysmally ineffective and morally destructive.

But education about sexual matters should no more be dismissed out of hand due to its associations than the office of pastor should be abolished because of the indiscretions of a few, than churches should be closed because of the bad press from religious cults, than motherhood should be banned due to the increase of "prom moms."

True sex education should be based on the truth of God's Word. A theology of sexuality should begin with the Scriptures and end with the Scriptures. There is nothing wrong with a theology of sex; there is everything right with it. Would to God that every young person in America could embrace these lofty principles *before* marriage. If not then, certainly after marriage. But at some point all believers need to conform to these life-changing concepts.

Why are these things not being taught today? Why is the church ignoring the problem? Why are parents reluctant to teach their children? In part, I feel, it is because we have associated sex education with its worst elements and have concluded that sex education is the domain of the world dedicated to the demoralization of our youth.

I submit that the church should reclaim its rightful place as the *"pillar and ground of the truth"* and teach all the truth. Doctrines of sex are every bit as much a part of the Bible as other truths. The Bible's emphasis is away from plumbing and practice to a godly and honorable philosophy built on sound theology.

Once a sound theology of sexuality is acquired, the marriage can be freed from its Corinthian past and have a solid foundation upon which to build a ministry of sexuality.

[1] Ed Wheat and Gaye Wheat, *Intended for Pleasure* (Old Tappan, N.J.: Fleming H. Revell Co., 1977), 18.

[2] Wheat, 18.

[3] John White, *Eros Redeemed* (Downers Grove, Ill.: InterVarsity Press, 1993), 41.

[4] Wheat, 18-19.

[5] Kenneth S. Wuest, *Philippians Through the Revelation* (Grand Rapids, Mich.: Wm. B. Eerdmans Publishing Co., 1959), 140.

[6] Tim Stafford, "Getting Serious About Lust in an Age of Smirks," *Journal of Biblical Counseling* 13, no 3 (1995): 4-5.

[7] Neil T. Anderson, *A Way of Escape* (Eugene, Oreg.: Harvest House Publishers, 1994), 67.

[8] Paul David Tripp, "The Way of the Wise: Teaching Teenagers About Sex," *Journal of Biblical Counseling* 13, no 3 (1995): 39.

18

THE RENEWED VISION

There once lived a cowboy preacher in the old West who was led by God to start a church in a dusty cow town. He converted an abandoned saloon into a chapel, dismantling the bar and using the wood to fashion some crude benches and a rustic pulpit. Wanting his congregation to gain a burden for the lost, he used the leftover wood to lovingly carve the letters to form a verse to nail over the exit door. It read, "Where there is no vision, the people perish." The former bar became known far and wide as a soul-changing outpost, and many lives were transformed. Prostitutes, alcoholics, petty thieves, and other incorrigible sinners knelt on rough-hewn floorboards and poured out tearful prayers for deliverance. The church was packed each service and the windows reverberated with the sounds of joyful praise to God.

Soon the faithful pastor was called to a new field. He was confident though, that all would be well. After a tearful departure, he rode out of a town in which hymns had replaced bawdy barroom choruses and street witnesses had replaced streetwalkers.

Some time passed, and the preacher's travels brought him near his former church. Desiring to renew old friendships, he dropped in for a visit. As he rode down the familiar street, his spirit was strangely unsettled within him. Something was wrong. He realized why when he came within sight of the church building, once again boarded over and empty of life. He dismounted, then pried away the boards. As he surveyed the familiar room, he saw that dust covered the old benches and pulpit. Well-worn hymnbooks littered the floor amidst broken window glass.

His heart was broken as he searched for an answer. How had the church sunk to such a state of decay? "Why, God?" he pleaded. "What has happened to this church that was once so very much alive?" When he lifted his head, he had his answer. There above the door were the wooden letters he had so lovingly carved years before, and there was the verse just as he remembered it—with one notable exception. One letter had fallen to the floor, drastically changing the message: the letter "w" was missing and it now read, "_here there is no vision, the people perish."

Somehow the church had lost its original vision. They stopped winning souls and grew cold toward spiritual things. The gospel light had been extinguished and the hope of salvation had been removed from the landscape. The church had died because their vision had died.

Many ministries suffer from the same malady; moms and dads lose their vision for parenting, Sunday school teachers lose their vision for teaching, and Christians lose their vision for service in general.

It is no different for the Christian marriage. The original glow of love slowly dims, and the enthusiasm of youthful idealism fades. Many marriages shed tears over dusty recollections from a distant past. They wonder what has happened. They don't realize that they have lost their vision, and they fail to see that when the vision dies, the marriage follows suit.

A renewed vision is what is needed. If the inner man is not renewed day by day, hardness of heart and carnality set in. The psalmist prayed, *"Wilt thou not revive us again: that thy people may rejoice in thee?"* (Ps. 85:6). The same is true for virtually every area of the Christian life. We need renewed strength (Isa. 40:31), a renewed mind (Rom 12:2), and a renewed spirit (Ps. 51:10). The apostle Paul recognized this need of a renewed vision in our love relationships. He prayed for the Thessalonian believers that they would *"increase and abound"* in their love (I Thess. 3:12-13).

The reason for this need is our tendency to lose the original vision that so motivated us at the beginning of our ministries. What parent can forget holding his first child with fear and trembling as the weight of responsibility pressed upon him? But how easy for that sense of awe to weaken after the terrible twos and during the teen years. What teacher or preacher of the gospel didn't begin with a vision of changing a soul and transforming the world? What believer can forget the excitement of conversion and the vision of loved ones experiencing the same joy? And what husband or wife did not once embrace the dream of an intimate spiritual fellowship with one another in the love of God?

But dreams fade and visions die in even the most committed of hearts. Sin hardens us, sin deceives us, the flesh misleads us, and Satan blinds us. Unless we fan the flame of devotion committed to us, we can be overcome by darkness.

The reasons for this spiritual declension vary, but they result in the same coldness in our relationships with one another as in our relationship with God.

We become problem conscious rather than power conscious. Whereas once we saw only Christ across the water, we now see the boisterous winds and threatening waves. When circumstances and problems assail us, we begin to believe that there is no way out. The problems loom so big before us and the challenges seem so overwhelming in light of our own strength that our hearts melt in fear and our spirits dry up in despair.

We also focus on human ability rather than divine power. In Luke 5 Peter was skeptical about the possibility of catching any fish because he had already tried every trick in his manual for professional fishermen. All his skill, his experience, and his tested equipment had failed. Even a marathon fishing trip, during which he applied all the secrets of the trade, failed to produce any fruit. When Christ exhorted him to try one more time, he protested, *"We have toiled all the night, and have taken nothing"* (v. 5). But in order to placate the Lord, he grudgingly agreed to make one last try, *"nevertheless at thy word I will let down the net."* (Christ had told him to go all out and let down all his nets). Peter's reluctance was traceable to a comparison of the challenge before him to the ability within him. He had failed to factor in God's power.

Peter was also fixated on natural laws rather than supernatural miracles. He assumed that because there were no fish in the area or because they were not biting, there was nothing more to be done. He did not fully believe that Christ could change all that.

A couple who have lost their vision for their marriage often believes the same. They have tried all the seminars, read all the books, and applied the latest techniques of communication. They have studied hints on how to spice up their sex life and embraced the latest pop psychology taught by the popular Dr. Feel Good, but they have seen no change. They have concluded that if none of this works, then nothing works. They believe that change is humanly impossible. They are right! *"With men this is impossible."* And it is impossible because marriage is at its core a spiritual relationship. Spiritual relationships don't respond well to carnal techniques. That's the bad news. The good news is that *"with God all things are possible"* (Matt. 19:26). When God's supernatural power is applied to natural problems, the result is miraculous!

Peter could not see this. He was fixated on his failure. He was focused on his lack of success despite his best efforts. He was blinded to the future because he was bound to the past. He had *"taken nothing"* and was discouraged and embarrassed because, after all, he was a professional.

There are enough failures in most marriages to discourage and embarrass us as well. Every marital house has a closet or two with a skeleton in it that the Devil enjoys pulling out on occasion. He delights in reserving this exercise for the times that you are just beginning to feel the stirrings of new hope. Then he rushes to the closet, jerks it open, and dangles the skeleton of past failure in your face. "You see this?" he demands. "Do you really believe that you can ever overcome this?" When he reminds you that sin abounds, you need to remind him that *"where sin abounded, grace did much more abound"* (Rom. 5:20).

Satan, the great *"accuser,"* devotes his inexhaustible energy to condemning you. He accuses you *"before our God day and night"* (Rev. 12:10), and he discourages you with every lie that his demented mind can conjure up. As the father of lies, his ingenuity knows no bounds; the variety of his lies, their subtle shades and obscured nuances, defy the imagination. They are all designed toward a predictable end: to discourage and defeat you.

These lies must be identified and attacked with the truth, and the greatest truth is *"greater is he that is in you, than he that is in the world"* (I John 4:4). Unfortunately, it is this very truth of the greatness of God that is often overlooked. Peter certainly missed it. He had respect for Christ, even calling Him *"Master"* (Luke 5:5), but he failed to see Him as He truly was. A similar low view of God is a common denominator in failed marriages. This image of God affects every aspect of a relationship and few realize it. A. W. Tozer writes, "The low view of God entertained almost universally among Christians is the cause of a hundred lesser evils everywhere among us. A whole new philosophy of the Christian life has resulted from this one basic error in our religious thinking."[1]

In the great passage on marriage (Eph. 5), I found twenty references to God in only sixteen verses. I was amazed to discover that in this brief passage, God is everywhere! "How did I fail to see this!" I asked myself.

The filling of the Spirit, the fear of God, and the example of Christ permeate the teaching on the subject of marriage. And yet, for many couples, God is the place of last resort. They believe that there are other methods and resources to be tried, and if all else fails, God is there if they need Him.

They need to ponder the question of the apostle Paul: *"Are ye so foolish? having begun in the Spirit, are ye now made perfect by the flesh?"* (Gal 3:3).

As a godly marriage should begin in the Spirit, it should continue in the Spirit. Any such continuation must include lifting our understanding of God to new and life-changing heights. As we understand Christ's trust in the Father even through the agony of the cross, we learn to trust Him in our disappointments. As we see His love for the church, we learn to love our mate. As we see His forgiveness, we have a model for forgiving our marriage partner.

Peter eventually came to see God clearly; in verse 5 he called Him *"Master,"* but by verse 8, he called Him *"Lord."* What made the difference? Peter had obeyed and in his obedience God had revealed Himself. His obedience was less than perfect, to be sure, but God honored it nonetheless. Despite a reluctant obedience and a weak faith, Peter had obeyed, and from his obedience sprang a new and vibrant vision.

God does not require a perfect faith to produce a miracle, only a partial one. The father who came to Christ pleading for the healing of his demoniac son admitted that his faith was not strong. Initially, he even approached Christ with some reservations about His ability to heal: *"If thou canst do any thing, have compassion on us, and help us"* (Mark 9:22). He wasn't absolutely convinced, only partially.

Maybe you've begun to wonder about God's power to help as well. When the problems get so serious and continue for so long, it is tempting to yield to the thoughts of doubt or to cave in to the torment of despair. Despite the mountain of fear towering over you, if you can find some faith, even a miniscule portion, God can use it. The disciples were discouraged because they had been unable to deliver the man's demon-possessed son. They asked Christ, *"Why could not we cast him out?"* Jesus quickly answered their question: *"Because of your unbelief"* but quickly assured them that unbelief could be displaced by even a little belief. *"If ye have faith as a grain of mustard seed, ye shall say unto this mountain,*

Remove hence to yonder place; and it shall remove; and nothing shall be impossible unto you" (Matt. 17:20). How big is your faith? You may say, "I don't seem to have much right now," and that's okay because not much is needed. Just a little bit.

The father of the demon-possessed boy had only a little faith, but he used it: *"Lord, I believe."* He then asked for God to make up for his lack of faith: *"Help thou mine unbelief"* (Mark 9:24). God is not looking for a mountain of belief, only a mustard seed of faith. He doesn't demand perfect faith; partial faith will do. Do you have that much? Whatever you have, use it. Whatever God says to do, do it. He will honor your obedience.

While writing this chapter, God was gracious to bring me good news of the power of renewed vision. I have been blessed to learn that two of the "alumni" couples of our counseling ministry are prospering in their recovery from near fatal wounds to their marriages.

One of them came to me some time ago reeling from the aftershock of an affair. The future was bleak, their relationship teetering on the brink of annihilation. No one would have given this couple much hope a short time ago. Their own vision was dimmed and their faith reduced to almost nothing. But almost nothing was enough! I recently sat with them and heard the story of their recovery work and their gradual climb out of the slough of despond. They had faithfully worked at the follow-up program I had assigned and had grown in their love for God and for each other. Now, they wanted to know how to get back into the saddle of usefulness for God. The God of all hope had promised them a new beginning and had delivered. *"Behold, I will do a new thing; now it shall spring forth; shall ye not know it? I will even make a way in the wilderness, and rivers in the desert"* (Isa. 43:19).

I also received a call from a pastor friend who had acted as the follow-up agent and mentor for another couple whose marriage had withstood not only the shock of perversion and immorality but also widespread public exposure. The pastor related how this couple had faithfully adhered to their program and over the years had become faithful and fruitful members of his flock. He had visited them in their home and had personally witnessed the love and devotion they now shared for one another. Their love is not only restored but has returned with a roar! Truly the Lord had made them to *"increase and abound"* in it (I Thess. 3:12). And He can do the same for you!

The cure for the empty heart and abandoned hearth is the same as that of the empty and dusty converted saloon in the cow town. The letter "w" needs to be reattached to the wall.

---

[1] A.W. Tozer, *The Knowledge of the Holy* (New York: Harper and Brothers, 1961), 6.

ABOUT THE AUTHOR

Jim Binney is a noted author, broadcaster, Bible conference speaker, and biblical counselor. He has taught in various Bible colleges and seminaries as an adjunct professor and has chaired the graduate division of Biblical counseling in one of them.

He is currently the head of Shepherd's Care Ministries International based in Manila, Philippines where he lives with his wife Maria. There he directs a counseling center, serves as lead counselor and trains others in counseling.

He also has an active ministry of training and equipping Asian pastors from several countries and islands around the region. He can be reached at www.shepherdscareint.com.

CPSIA information can be obtained
at www.ICGtesting.com
Printed in the USA
BVHW071037050720
582985BV00005B/274